This Patch of Earth

This Patch of Earth

Observations on a Rural Life

Daryln Brewer Hoffstot

STACKPOLE
BOOKS

Essex, Connecticut

STACKPOLE BOOKS
An imprint of Globe Pequot Publishing Group, Inc.
64 South Main Street
Essex, CT 06426
www.globepequot.com

"An Avian Murder Case on a Quiet Back Porch" was published in *The New York Times* on June 2, 2023

"What You Discover When You Garden at Night" was published in *The New York Times* on August 8, 2023

"What a Search for the Signs of Spring Reveals" was published in *The New York Times* on March 23, 2024

"A Fading Tree, Once Majestic, Had to Come Down. But It Wasn't the End." was published in *The New York Times* on October 16, 2024

"Dreams of the Possible and Impossible for This Year's Garden" was published in *The New York Times* on March 28, 2025

"What Things Left Behind Say About a Home's Past, and the Times We Live In" was published in *The New York Times* on October 11, 2025

"What My Dog Taught Me About Aging" originally appeared as "As My Dog Grows Old, So Do I" in the Ideas section of *The Boston Globe* on January 22, 2024

"Digging Basil's Grave" originally appeared in the Ideas section of *The Boston Globe* on July 4, 2024

"Thanksgiving" originally appeared in the Ideas section of *The Boston Globe* on November 2025

"What I Learned from My Compost Heap" originally appeared in *The Philadelphia Inquirer* on November 16, 2023

"When the Rains Come" originally appeared in *The Philadelphia Inquirer* on May 3, 2024

"In Praise of a Garden" originally appeared in *Horticulture Magazine*, November/December 2024

"An Ode on Snow Days" originally appeared as "An Ode to Snow Days—and Why They Really Matter" in the *Hartford Courant* on February 25, 2024

All other essays first appeared in *Pittsburgh Quarterly*

All illustrations by Getty Creative except images for "The Springhouse" courtesy of Eric Sloane Family Trust.

British Library Cataloguing in Publication Information available

Library of Congress Cataloging-in-Publication Data available
ISBN 978-0-8117-7829-9 (cloth)
ISBN 978-0-8117-7830-5 (ebook)

for my family, always

Be still and listen to the voices that belong
To the streambanks and the trees and the open fields.
There are songs and sayings that belong to this place,
By which it speaks for itself and no other.

—FROM "A POEM ON HOPE,"
BY WENDELL BERRY

Contents

Acknowledgments

Thank you to my first readers, often critical, always kind. You make my essays better.

So does Douglas Paul Alteen, my editor at *The New York Times*, for which I am grateful.

And there are many reasons to thank Doug Heuck, who has published my column in *Pittsburgh Quarterly* for many years.

I appreciate the continued support of Judith Schnell, my book editor at Stackpole Books and Jed Lyons of the Globe Pequot Publishing Group, who encouraged my writing long ago.

I am indebted to the ornithologists, plant ecologists, entomologists, mycologists, ethnobotanists, foresters, and others who know far more than I about the natural world and who share their knowledge so willingly.

Thank you to Corey Snyder, who drove an hour and a half to look at a dead maple tree and turned that tree into beautiful bowls, which have now traveled the world.

I could not have written this book without my family, or my dear friends.

Also by Daryln Brewer Hoffstot:

A Farm Life: Observations from Fields and Forests

Introduction

I've been thinking a lot lately about our western Pennsylvanian landscape and the language we use to describe it, and I found inspiration in a surprising place—a book about the Gaelic language called *Thirty-Two Words for Field: Lost Words of the Irish Landscape*, by Manchan Magan. Magan tells us that there are thirty-two Gaelic words for one of our English words: *field*, for instance. In Gaelic, *branar* is a fallow field and *cuibhewann* is a field tilled in partnership with a neighbor. *Plasog* is a sheltered field in which a mare would foal. *Abuaile* is a field for keeping cattle before milking and *chthairin* is a field with a fairy dwelling in it. There are twenty-five additional words in Gaelic for our word, *field*.

Magan believes these old Irish words are gifts from the ancient past, that they ground us and remind us that we are connected to all things—to fields, hawks, and fairies. And in Ireland, fairies connect people deeply to their environment, so much so that one cannot build a house on a fairy ring. The locals know where those fairy rings are located and such land is strictly protected from human intervention—a fairy conservancy of sorts.

I have a great deal of respect for fairies. In an essay I wrote about the elder trees on our farm, I made sure not to get on the bad side of the spirits that are supposed to live near that tree. Elder trees come with many myths—the druids thought the tree holy, and in more modern times in *Harry Potter and the Deathly Hallows*, the most powerful wand in the world was made from the elder tree. If you cut an elder branch, one myth says, you must be on bended knee with hands folded to avoid the wrath of the "Elder Mother." You can bet I was on bended knee when I cut a branch to observe its hollow center, such branches having been used by ancient cultures to make into flutes, whistles, and maple syrup spiles.

Only now are we understanding in this country what the Greeks and Romans understood way before us—the health benefits of the elderberry. The berry is said to help with so many ailments that Hippocrates called the tree "a medicine chest." Is that a myth? I don't think so. Native Americans have long used elder for food and medicine. Herbalists recognize its power and Missouri grows it for research. Yet in Pennsylvania, we try to eradicate the tree. It is a weedy looking thing, not trim and compact, and PennDOT sprays the roadsides where elder is likely to grow.

But why, you ask, am I going on about fairies and ancient cultures and the Gaelic words they use in Ireland? I don't live in Ireland. I live in western Pennsylvania, where my stories are set. But I take a cue from the Irish here—to listen to the natural world, to give voice to the landscape, the birds, bees, bugs, mammals, weeds, and the native plants that we have *here*. To learn the legends and folklore and find the vernacular that best describes our geography, the land on which *we* all live. Maybe even to listen to fairies.

I try to understand what is happening to these plants and animals and say it to others in a way that makes sense. To slow down, observe and record, to create a language about our western Pennsylvania landscape. "Nature is a language," Ralph Waldo Emerson wrote. "And every new fact one learns is a new word."

I try to give a nod to the ancient peoples who came before us, not only the Celts as in Ireland, but our Native Americans, who know so much more about our earth than we do and who offer us their stories and advice if only we would listen. The Cherokee call trees "standing people." Native Americans know to eat only the ripe, yellow fruit of the mayapple, minus the seeds; the rest of the plant is poisonous. They know how to use stinging nettle to help with arthritis and other ailments. (The Irish also believe that three meals of boiled nettles before the end of May purifies the blood and assures good health.)

In Pennsylvania, many people try to eradicate nettles too—think of them as weeds. To quote Ralph Waldo Emerson again: "What is a weed? A plant whose virtues have not yet been discovered." But nettles' virtues have long been discovered. An herbalist told me, "Nettles are one of the most nutrient dense herbs we have, full of vitamins, minerals, and antioxidants, and far tastier than spinach."

We do have our own language here. We call apples that fruit in summer "July apples." An apple expert in Maine told me that "July apple" is a local nickname—one he'd never heard before. We call a certain morel mushroom, one of the first to emerge in spring from the forest floor, a rubberneck. Some call ginseng, sang. Ramps are called wild leeks or the ransom. We have ramp festivals in Pennsylvania. We tap maple trees so we have the language of maple sugaring, and we call a break in the mountain a "gap." We might call our lowlands "hollers" and our streams "cricks." I grew up calling the thorns on plants "prickers," but western Pennsylvanians call them "jaggers."

Landscape and language that are married to each other.

Local lore says it will be a mild winter if paper wasp nests hang low to the ground and the more black on a woolly caterpillar the harsher the winter. A friend says if there is a cloud bank over Laurel Ridge that a "storm's a brewing," and our babysitter used to say she could hear "the ridge roar." The last snow of the year, she said, is called "onion snow" because that's when we should plant onions. I followed animal tracks one winter day to pay witness to those creatures with which I share this small patch of earth. Those animals are not everywhere, but they are here, in our backyards, their tracks a language in themselves.

A local friend who grew up here, a deer hunter for his whole life, told me bad luck comes to anyone who shoots an albino deer. I have seen only one albino deer in thirty-seven years and it was so shocking I pulled the car over, stopped, and stared. My husband was on horseback when he saw an albino deer and he was so confused by the different coloring he was sure it was a goat. My friend's father refused to shoot the albino deer, but then a fellow they knew did, and killed it. The myth was shattered because the next day the fellow who shot the deer hit the lottery and won $100,000. But within a month he'd had a heart attack, and according to my friend, has had health problems ever since. Perhaps we western Pennsylvanians do believe in fairies?

Is it our imagination? Maybe. But I think that fairies and myths and superstition somehow bring us closer to the natural world, give us a bigger stake in it, perhaps make us care about it more, might even make us more inclined to save it.

We now have in our woods a sad story about our ancient ash tree—a tree once used to make baseball bats, an American pastime if there ever was one. And that story is that we allowed into this country, from Asia, a bright green beetle—the emerald ash borer—and that beetle has decimated our Pennsylvania forests as we had come to know them.

For an essay on native plants, I learned that chickadees feed their babies six to nine thousand caterpillars for the two weeks the babies are in the nest. That's one species, and one brood, in one year. That fact—those words, that story—made me rethink the role of caterpillars in our ecosystem; I'll never look at caterpillars the same way again.

One of my favorite stories was about the chimney swift—a bird that never alights until it tucks itself into our nineteenth-century chimney at night. And I love the fact that women did much of the research on chimney swifts in the nineteenth century—a story of women and birds. Why? Because the women were at home, while the men were out in factories or in fields, and it was the women who bonded with these small torpedo-shaped birds that lived in their chimneys. And why did the birds live in chimneys? Because we'd cut down the old growth trees that had once been their home—and their name was changed from the American swift to chimney swift. Their numbers are down 70 percent nationwide.

Or the kingfisher, one of my all-time favorite birds. I love to watch them dive every summer across the pond and listen to their rattling call. The kingfisher has all sorts of Native American myths surrounding it, some positive, others negative, but the one I prefer to apply to our little valley here is that the kingfisher represents peace and prosperity.

Or snapping turtles that everyone loves to hate and with which they make turtle soup here, yet snapping turtles are so important to our Pennsylvania ponds. They keep our ponds clean by eating carrion and consume vegetation that balances the ecosystem for fish, birds, and dragonflies—and dragonflies eat lots of mosquitos.

And the story of an eastern phoebe, a bird that has nested every year on the light fixture outside our pantry door, a bird being attacked, I believe, by the house sparrow, a bird we introduced to this country in the 1850s to control caterpillars.

Or the stories of the floods we now get on the farm living as we do at the base of three hills. What was once the 100-year flood now comes three or four times a year, a story of our changing climate.

I tried to tell the story of our Pennsylvania bats, but so few are left on our farm now. Where we once had many flying overhead at dusk, last summer when I closed the chicken coop, I saw two each night (up from one the year before). Ninety-nine percent of Pennsylvania bats have been killed by white-nose syndrome, a fungus that we likely moved unknowingly on our shoes, clothing, or outdoor gear from caves in Europe or Asia around 2006.

And, of course, we Pennsylvanians are most blessed with the language and stories of Rachel Carson, who lived her early life nearby on the Allegheny River and warned us of environmental hazards—her words having sadly come true across the world.

These are some of the words and stories of our Appalachian landscape, of our place, our lives, and I wonder, like Scheherazade—the fictional character in the Middle Eastern tale *One Thousand and One Nights* who tells a story to the king each night to save her life—if we keep telling these stories, might we also save our planet?

I was disappointed when I read a book edited by Barry Lopez and Debra Gwartney called *Home Ground: A Guide to the American Landscape*, where such landscapes as dunes, avalanches, and glaciers are described by forty-five writers about the places they live—and there is not one entry from western Pennsylvania. Writers from Cape Cod, Iowa, Montana, North Carolina, Maine, and Alaska, but none from here. The closest we get is southern Appalachia and that is not us.

What are the lost words of our Pennsylvania landscape? If we look at our fields, how do we describe them? The field where we keep our cows? The field where we cut hay? The field my husband and daughter like to gallop across? The field where last summer I saw a killdeer? I think it is time we give thought to the words that describe what we have here, that tell our stories.

I shudder to think what my words and my stories would be if I were a writer today living in Pacific Palisades—a landscape loved by those who live there. Or recently in Asheville, North Carolina, or Louisiana after Hurricane Katrina, or New York City after Hurricane Sandy, and so many other places being destroyed by fire or flood or drought. The hottest year on record was 2024. How should we tell those stories? Environmental writers everywhere are asking this question.

I feel lucky to live in a green valley surrounded by two ridges of the Appalachians, in a place largely unchanged for many years. And I think of two wise men, two of our first environmentalists: Aldo Leopold, who said, "the oldest task in human history—to live on a piece of land without spoiling it." And Henry David Thoreau, who said, "A man is rich in proportion to the number of things he can afford to let alone." We must try to be good stewards of our land.

Many people have told me they think my first book, *A Farm Life*, was a love letter to my family and they are correct. *This Patch of Earth* is too, but both are also love letters to the land on which I live—an appreciation and a devotion to what we have in western Pennsylvania. How grateful I am to have raised my family in a spot of such beauty and abundance.

One of my favorite trees on the farm was a big, old maple, which was dying, and I wrote about its demise in 2022 for *The New York Times*. Eventually, we had to take it down—it broke my heart—but I wrote a follow-up story that appeared in that newspaper in October 2024. But, that story ended on a happy note because Corey Snyder, a local woodturner, made the tree into beautiful bowls. As much as I miss that beautiful, old tree—and I see her still every time

I walk out to the side yard—at least she has a second life, not just here, where she put down her deep roots, but across our country.

Five hundred and sixty-seven *New York Times* readers from places such as Canada, Colorado, Vermont, and Italy wrote and told me about their maples, hickories, apple trees, sequoias, oaks, and horse chestnuts. They responded to the language that described our landscape—words not about fields, but about our trees, the native species we have growing here, which are filled with bird nests and give us shade and beauty and maple syrup. Their responses gave me hope, not just that people care about trees, but that they feel grounded to the land on which they live—which, in my opinion, is the only thing that can save us.

FLORA, FAUNA, AND FUNGI

A Fading Tree, Once Majestic, Had to Come Down. But It Wasn't the End.

When you live a long time with trees, they become a part of you.

So it pained me to take down the old sugar maple, one rafter at a time, my arboreal cathedral, her demise not due to flames, but an underground blaze of mycelium. Small honey-colored mushrooms fruiting at her base were "the giveaway," said the forester.

The tree was old when we moved to the farm thirty-six years ago, about the age of this farmhouse—160 years, we figured. I know she was here as far back as the 1940s because we have a photo of her in her younger days, much smaller and not quite ruling over the side yard as she did in her later years.

In her old age, she reached about ninety feet high. And she was a tree with a personality. Not straight and narrow, but quirky, with a trunk that had split into four and branches that splayed this way and that, coping with aging as best she could. I felt privileged to have lived under her canopy for many years.

But lately she's been battered by torrential rains and then drought. Summers are hotter, winters aren't as cold. She's had little snow cover to insulate her roots. Climate change probably made her more susceptible to the fungus, armillaria, the forester said.

And she's not the only tree stressed on the farm. Ash trees have been decimated by the emerald ash borer. Native dogwoods are dying of anthracnose. Hemlocks are being attacked by the hemlock woolly adelgid, and spicebush and sassafras are suffering from laurel wilt, spread by the nonnative ambrosia beetle. Woods that were once woods are becoming fields again.

We watched the old maple die slowly. She's not doing well, my husband and I said to each other.

Then, in one season, her entire left side started coming down. Limbs crashed onto the springhouse below, chunks of bark everywhere. Anthills appeared at her base. Vegetation that had lodged high in her crevices looked less vigorous to me.

Even the birds were leaving. I saw no Baltimore oriole nest high in her branches as I had the year before, nor did I find on the ground the glossy white and elliptical egg of a mourning dove. Perhaps the birds knew that securing a nest to those branches was no longer safe.

Still, I hoped we could save her. Prune the dead limbs. Trim back. A little longer, I begged. I knew I was too attached to her. My children had grown up beside her. Animals of all sorts scampered about her trunk. Black bears ambled by. At night from the sleeping porch, I watched the moon circle east to west above her. She was more than just a tree, she was a village.

And what, I wondered, had she witnessed in her long life? Horse and buggy, farmers who lived in log houses with corn cob chinking, a barn raising, cold

winters with piles of snow, many more birds, more insects, lots of bats (which are almost gone from the farm now). Darker skies, brighter stars, years with no airplane noise and then Flight 93 hijacked overhead. She'd watched the pond being dug, the house modernized, the land altered, by us, to divert new floodwaters. Like the wrinkles on my face, her gnarly roots were a record of years gone by, of lives lived, the blessed and the painful.

But I could fool myself no longer. It had become too dangerous to walk underneath her or mow the grass. My husband and another fellow strung ropes to her branches. I could feel it in my limbs. I didn't want to look. They used pole pruners and chain saws: dangerous, noisy work. They were experienced, but not on this scale. We had to call in a professional with a bucket truck, more people and more powerful chain saws. But he was so busy dealing with dead and diseased trees in our small town that he said he'd drop her, but not clean up the mess.

She was down.

That couldn't be the end, though. I remembered the suggestions of many readers of my original *New York Times* essay who urged me to turn the old maple into tables, shelves, lumber, guitars, or bowls. I took their advice.

"Turn it, don't burn it," says Corey Snyder's business card. I'd met Snyder, a woodturner, years ago at our farmer's market, had bought beautiful bowls from him as wedding gifts. I asked if he could do the same with our tree. He said he'd come look at the wood. Maple is often a light wood, sometimes almost white, he said, which many people don't like. But he was willing to see how the grain turned out.

His chain saw struck up another chorus. More piles of sawdust accumulated on the grass. This time, I put my nose to the newly cut grain and soaked in its sweet smell. We placed heavy chunks of the tree into a tractor bucket, then loaded them onto his trailer. He took them back to his shop. He'd let me know if the wood was worth using.

A couple months later, Snyder presented me with three beautiful, honey-colored bowls: one for our son, one for our daughter, and one for us. Each has different characteristics. One has a "bark inclusion," a dark brown mushroom-shaped mark where a branch had been trimmed or damaged.

Another has a wave pattern resulting from a Y (a crotch, Snyder called it) where two branches met and the tree's growth pattern changed. One has light streaks of green because of mineral deposits. The bowls are different shapes, sizes, and thicknesses. I asked him how he chose what form the bowls should take. "I let the piece of wood dictate," he said.

The old maple had spoken.

She still had not revealed her age, though. I had hoped I could count her rings, but she was so scuffed up with a kaleidoscope of chain saw marks that it was impossible to do so.

Now, instead of gazing up at the tree, I can hold her in my hands. The bowls are silky smooth, not rough like her bark, light-colored, not dark, small, not stately. But they are the old maple in a second life, albeit a different form. Some of her will stay here, where she put down deep roots, but other parts will venture out into a wider world because Snyder said he liked working with the wood so much he wants to cut more.

Pretty soon only the stump will remain. I console myself further that, over time, the stump will become another little ecosystem unto itself. Bacteria will decompose the wood, ants and beetles will move in, and then perhaps pileated woodpeckers, which feed on them. Salamanders may shelter there, snakes hibernate, and chipmunks hide acorns in her crevices. Fungi, moss, and lichen will grow and nutrients will return to the soil. Maybe, someday, a seedling will sprout.

Yet when I walk out to the side yard, I still see her standing, her long, elegant branches reaching skyward. It is autumn now and there is no longer that colorful array of red, yellow, and orange leaves blanketing the ground beneath her. And last spring, I strained to hear the dawn chorus.

That glorious sound is not as close to the house as it once was, not as vibrant. It emanates from branches farther away, from trees closer to the forest. The birds that once called the old maple home have had to move on, to sing elsewhere. So must I.

The Common Snapping Turtle

I think it is a rule that people inevitably destroy what they do not understand.

—Wendell Berry

Each spring before my first real swim (I have dipped every month of the year, but that doesn't count as a real swim), I stand at the house and gaze downhill to the pond. I scan the water's surface, looking for snapping turtles. I see them come up for air—their little nostrils, at the tip of their snouts, acting as snorkels. I don't know if they overwintered in the mud at the bottom of the pond or made their way across land, but I always hope they aren't there.

They always are.

Maybe if I'm quiet and they don't see me, they won't bother me, I think. Towel in hand, I tiptoe to the pond, but no matter how stealthily I creep, they see me before I'm halfway. They swim away as fast as their prehistoric legs can muster—the only proof of their presence the ripples they leave behind.

All they ask of me, of any human, is to leave them alone.

I haven't always done so.

When we first moved to the farm, I believed what I'd heard about snapping turtles. That they'd bite off my toes or fingers while I swam in the pond. Snatch mallard ducklings from the water's surface, drag them under, and gobble them up. I was so afraid that I allowed a farmer neighbor to catch a snapping turtle and make turtle soup. I've caught turtles too—by dangling chicken necks attached to empty milk jugs floating atop the water—and relocated them to new homes.

That's when the snapping turtle hissed and its powerful jaws lashed out at me. Who can blame it? I had taken this ancient creature, which has been roaming the earth for about ninety million years and can live to be one hundred, away from its home and family. I am ashamed to write this.

And I'm not the only one afraid of what lurks in the muck. Over the years I've had to coax countless people into the pond with me. They are scared of snakes and turtles. But what we didn't know is that snapping turtles don't usually attack in water. They might if we stepped on one in the muck—which is why I jump off the dock—but in years of swimming in our pond, I've never even been brushed by one. Where snapping turtles do attack is on land—where they're out of their element and feel threatened by the likes of me. Then they'll strike.

"The vile temperament associated with these reptiles largely results from provocation by human beings, the latter making the situation confrontational," wrote David Carroll in his book *The Year of the Turtle*. "If cornered, approached or restrained, the turtle will lash out with legendary speed and terrific force, its head and neck becoming lethal weapons," Carroll said.

Still, contrary to popular belief, snapping turtles can't sever a finger, though they can inflict a pretty good wound, Carroll said. "Snapping turtles lived more harmoniously with dinosaurs than with humans."

Snapping turtles look scary. Their carapace—or upper shell—resembles armor. Their necks extend, their jaws are hooked, legs scaly, claws sharp, and tails long. (Their Latin name, *Chelydra serpentina*, means tortoise snake.) And they are big: usually weighing ten to thirty-five pounds, but can reach seventy-five pounds. Another reason they become aggressive, however, is that despite their size and power, their shells do not fully cover their bodies as on box turtles, for instance. The carapace is large—up to twenty inches in length—but the lower shell, the plastron, is small so they cannot fully protect themselves.

Snapping turtles may live a long time, but they can take fifteen to twenty years to successfully reproduce. Their eggs resemble ping pong balls with "a

white shell so tough that the egg may be bounced on a hard surface without breaking," according to *Turtles of the United States and Canada*, by Clifford H. Pope. Of the twenty to sixty eggs they lay each year, about 90 percent get eaten.

Snapping turtles know I'm walking across the lawn because they "have great eyesight and can sense vibration through their plastron, which acts as a sounding board," Carroll said. There's debate whether they hibernate or brumate, the latter meaning that on a warm day, they might wake up, crawl around, and have a drink. Whatever it's called, snapping turtles can go without air breathing for five and a half to six months; instead, they take up oxygen and dispel carbon dioxide from the throat and cloaca.

Reptile expert and iguana specialist Wendy Townsend said that snapping turtles, which are omnivores, are good for the health of our pond. "They consume a lot of vegetation, which helps balance the ecosystem for plants, fish, frogs, birds, insects, and dragonflies, the latter being great consumers of mosquitos," she said. Snapping turtles keep ponds clean by eating carrion. The Turtle Guardian website describes them as the "turkey-vultures of the lake." They also eat fish, frogs, snakes—and birds.

So will they eat all my ducklings?

"That's just not going to happen," Townsend said. "It's really about: Can they catch it?" Most carnivores, she said, won't expend the energy chasing something they can't catch. "They'll eat fish that are wounded—creatures that are slow, injured, or lagging behind—if they notice they have a different way of swimming, for instance."

Carroll agreed. They'll eat whatever they can get hold of, he said, but "only very rarely capture waterfowl or game fish, contrary to frequent reports." And, he reminded me—ducks coevolved with snapping turtles—and both are still here.

Snapping turtles have lots of predators too: mostly raccoons and skunks, but also coyotes, mink, crow, and fox. Of the 360 turtle species in the world, 187 are threatened with extinction. Pennsylvania's snappers are not, but its cousin to the south is: the alligator snapping turtle. The reasons include loss of habitat, pollution, water quality, the pet trade, and human consumption. Warnings exist now not to eat them. "Snapping turtles are what's called bio-accumulators," Carroll said, "which means they accumulate pesticides or heavy metals in their flesh."

Snapping turtles can wander for miles looking for good nesting sites or better habitat and often end up as roadkill. Townsend urges people to get snapping turtles off the road in any way possible. But be careful. The best way to pick up a turtle is at the back of the shell or by the thighs, but not by the tail, which used to be recommended. The tail is an extension of the vertebrae and can become dislocated that way. Carroll believes snapping turtles map their home territories with an internal compass, so never turn a turtle around. They know in which direction they want to go.

I mentioned to a friend over dinner that I was writing about snapping turtles and that I was sorry I'd caught and relocated them. Why, are they endangered, he asked? No, I said. Why feel bad, then, they are nasty creatures. How did he know that? I asked. Because in summer camp he used to poke them with boat oars.

I have thought about that exchange many times. In Canada, the common snapping turtle is of special concern and in 2017 the Ontario government banned the hunting of snapping turtles. Can the US be far behind? We can't wait until they are threatened to rally around them; we need to rally around all creatures that live among us.

"Snapping turtles have remarkably adapted to whatever the planet throws at them," Carroll said. "They even survived the big asteroid."

But will they survive us?

What Was That White Bird?

The first time I saw the white bird flying overhead I thought I'd gone slightly mad because large white birds are not common in this valley. I was riding my bike on a rural road between two cow fields, a herd of black angus eyeing me warily. I pedaled slowly, watching what I presumed was an exotic visitor, white birds of all sorts running through my mind: egrets, snowy owls, ibis, seagulls, whooping cranes, snow geese, and ptarmigans.

The next time I saw the bird, I turned around and rode in the direction I'd seen it fly. It soared across the road to a copse between the two fields and I found it perched high on a tree limb, regal and sure of itself, easy to spot against the bright green leaves. I stopped and marveled at its whiteness, thrilled to see what instinct told me was something special. I noticed it had a few brown patches. Then the bird took off in a gentle glide, swooping up and down on the thermals, presumably hunting for mice. The third time, I got off my bike and walked across a field where it roosted like a beacon atop a largely leafless tree. But I didn't get very far. It flew away, white on white against a cloudy sky.

I concluded the bird was a raptor of some sort because it flew like a red-tailed hawk, had a similarly shaped body, and was flying where red-tailed hawks are supposed to be—except that it was bright white. A gyrfalcon? I knew gyrfalcons were white, but that would be a rare winter visitor here and my sightings were in summer and fall. We have an osprey nest about six miles from here, but the bird I saw was whiter. It resembled most a white hawk, common in Texas and South and Central America. I was stumped.

After a good deal of sleuthing, I decided the bird must be a leucistic hawk—something I'd never heard of—indeed, a leucistic red-tailed hawk. Annie Lindsay, the bird banding manager at nearby Powdermill Nature Reserve, confirmed my final guess and told me a leucistic hawk had been reported in our area. "Good sighting," she said.

Leucism is a rare condition that causes an aberration in the pigment, or melanin, in birds' feathers. It's also a general term for atypical coloration in mammals, fish, amphibians, and reptiles. Albinos are all-white with pink eyes whereas leucistic animals may have patches of color and normal eyes. Piebald horses, for instance, are leucistic.

I was thrilled by the color variation I saw in the bird, but life in the wild can be extra challenging for leucistic creatures. Without camouflage, both predator and prey spot them more easily. Mating can be difficult as they may not be recognized by their own kind. Eyesight is often poor and skin more sensitive to light. Birds' feathers can be weaker and flight hindered. They often die young.

Leucism has long been considered genetic, but scientists are now questioning whether environmental factors play a role in certain aspects of leucism, including a condition called progressive graying. An article in *Birding* suggested that toxins in Utah's Great Salt Lake might have caused additional leucism in eared grebes. Nightjars that fed on berries around Chernobyl may have shown increased partial leucism and blackbirds in urban areas could express more leucism than rural birds.

Allison Shultz, an associate curator of ornithology at the Natural History Museum of Los Angeles County, believes there are probably genetic and environmental causes of leucism. "Anything that will change a bird's DNA," she said. Cancer-causing toxins that humans worry about are the same for birds, she told me; such toxins can affect a bird's general health, including its ability to produce the right colors. Every time a bird molts and grows new feathers, melanin cells have the chance of being degraded by environmental toxins such as radiation.

Still, there's much ornithologists don't know about leucism in birds so Shultz and Stepfanie Aguillon, who was a Stanford Science Fellow at Stanford University and is now at the University of California, Los Angeles, have asked the scientific community to give as much attention to atypical plumage as birders do. In an article published in *Ornithology*, they wrote, "The fascination of the birding public with the brilliant colors and patterns of birds means sightings of individuals with atypical plumage receive extraordinary attention. We suggest that these sightings should receive equal attention from the scientific community, as they could further our evolutionary understanding of bird color and patterning."

To do that, they need our help. They've asked birders to become community scientists, to photograph unusual coloration in birds and post such photos to websites such as iNaturalist and eBird. Fill in the comments section too, Shultz requested, which will make finding anomalies easier. They've also encouraged the scientific community to give community scientists the credit they deserve, including authorship in scientific papers. "People are essential," she said. "Without lots of eyes out here we can't know everything,"

I got lucky and saw a spectacular white bird that led me on a wonderful investigation, but it also made me understand that paying attention to atypical coloration in birds is yet another way I might help our declining bird population. And while the great sleuth Sherlock Holmes himself may never have investigated leucistic hawks, I'm going to give him the last word. In Arthur Conan Doyle's "The Adventure of the Blanched Soldier," the fictional detective said, "I see no more than you, but I have trained myself to notice what I see."

I'm going to try harder to notice what I see and, in the process, to assist ornithologists to better understand our beleaguered and quickly disappearing birds.

Chanterelles

We bought a small section of woods some years ago that came with treasures not spelled out in the purchase agreement: chanterelles. We had no idea the prized orange mushroom would fruit the following summer. I wasn't even positive what type of mushroom it was—I'd never foraged for chanterelles before—but after consulting my field guide, I was pretty positive they were chanterelles.

(Regarding mushroom identification, my husband balks at the words *pretty positive.*)

I admit I'm an amateur, despite the fact that I've been teaching myself about mushrooms since we moved to the farm many years ago. I've read enough to know that I never touch, no less pick and eat—barely inhale the air surrounding—a white, gilled mushroom. (It could be the deadly amanita.) I've identified puffballs, scarlet elf cups, chicken of the woods, stinkhorn, turkey tail, and other types of mushrooms—and I've eaten countless pieces of buttery toast slathered with sautéed morels, for which I foraged. So, I'd say I'm fairly confident foraging for morels.

(Regarding mushroom identification, my husband balks at the words *fairly confident.*)

OK, I am confident about morels.

Foraging for morels is far more challenging than chanterelles, however, for one basic reason: chanterelles fruit in basically the same spot every year, whereas morels do not. Too much or too little rain might change the timing of chanterelle fruiting, but not the location. My field guide states that chanterelles

Chanterelle mushroom EPS10

fruit from July to September, which is when I've found them here, and the book describes them as "orange to yellow," which is also true of ours: some yellower, others more orange. Chanterelles are found "especially along paths." Spot on! Too easy!

I've since found chanterelles all over the farm.

Once I established that the newly discovered mushrooms were chanterelles, I set out to identify the species. I guessed they were smooth chanterelles—*Cantharellus lateritius*—but I wasn't sure, so I asked a chanterelle expert, Rachel Swenie, PhD, of the University of Tennessee at Knoxville.

Identifying chanterelles can be tricky, Swenie said. "There are many species that look similar and within one species there can be a lot of variability." From a photo I sent her, she thought we had *Catharellus flavolateritius*, so I was half right: it was a smooth chanterelle, but *flavolateritius*, not *lateritius*, as the latter appears only in the Gulf Coast region of the US. Half right, unfortunately, should never be good enough in anyone's book regarding mushroom identification.

When identifying mushrooms, Swenie considers where the mushroom was collected and which trees were nearby. (I have found beautiful specimens in an oak grove.) She uses scientific methods that a layperson might not, such as measuring spore size under a microscope and conducting DNA sequencing. "It's like sleuthing," she said. "You take all the information and at the end see if it helps. It's rather difficult and takes a practiced eye."

Doing such tests enabled her to identify a European species of chanterelle unknown in North America. The mushroom was sent to her by a citizen scientist in Connecticut and it turned out to be an albino version of *Cantharellus cibarius*. "It was a very neat find," she said. "Earlier research had suggested all chanterelle species found in North America were unique to this continent and that *Cantharellus cibarius* was a strictly European species."

Chanterelles are ectomycorrhizal, meaning they form a symbiotic relationship with certain trees, such as oak, birch, beech, pine, fir, hemlock, and spruce. The mushroom is beneficial to the tree and the tree to the mushroom. "Chanterelles increase the surface area of the tree's root system underground and scavenge minerals in the soil, nutrients that the trees would have difficulty accessing, such as nitrogen and phosphorous," she explained. "The fungus transfers those nutrients to the tree and, in exchange, the tree sends some of the sugars it produces by photosynthesis to feed the fungus."

An unusual feature of the chanterelle is that it does not have true gills as some mushrooms do. Instead, it has wrinkles, or "gill-like folds," Swenie called

them. "You can rub the wrinkles off like clay," she said. True gills cannot be rubbed off.

Numerous mushrooms can be confused with chanterelles. The most common look-alike in our area is the poisonous jack-o-lantern mushroom. One key difference between the two, explained John Plischke, a mycologist and founding member of the Western Pennsylvania Mushroom Club, is that jack-o-lanterns grow on wood, not on the ground. Still, that can be confusing. "If the wood rots and grows underground, you might see grass instead of wood," he said. Another difference is that jack-o-lanterns grow in large clumps. "A dozen or so caps together," Plischke said. "One or two chanterelles might grow together, but not a big clump." Jack-o-lanterns also have real gills.

Jack-o-lanterns are bright orange like chanterelles, which may be the reason the two are often confused. But, Swenie said to be wary of using color when identifying any mushroom because color can vary depending on when the mushroom is picked. "A lot of stuff changes color with age and rain," she said.

Some foragers claim that chanterelles smell like apricots. I've smelled them—and I have a keen sense of smell—but I've never smelled apricots. "I don't smell apricots either," Plischke said. "Maybe a little fruity, or pleasant," he said, but no apricots. Swenie pointed out that older and waterlogged mushrooms might also smell different. "Smell is not necessarily a telltale sign," she said.

Other look-alikes include the "the false chanterelle," *Hygrophoropsis aurantiaca*, and the shaggy, scaly, or woolly chanterelle, *Turbinellus floccosus*. "None of these are closely related to one another, nor to chanterelles," Swenie said. "They just appear similar to chanterelles to the untrained eye." The only group closely related to chanterelles that may be mistaken for them are trumpet mushrooms, in the genus *Craterellus*, "sisters to chanterelles," Swenie called them. They are edible but are hollow down the middle, whereas "the interior of an edible chanterelle will be white and stringy, like string cheese," she said.

"Really, the best way to learn to distinguish each of these groups is to learn from someone who knows them," Swenie said. "Joining a local mycology club is often the best way to get this type of experience."

How to wash mushrooms is a topic that splits people into two groups: those who wash them in water and those who believe water dilutes the taste. Swenie recommends cleaning them with a soft brush, but she isn't against a quick swish with water. Just don't waterlog them. "I have done both and personally do not see much of a difference," she said. "It just depends on how tolerant one is of a little dirt. If the mushrooms are fresh, they will taste good either way."

Chanterelles should be stored in wax paper or a brown paper bag in the refrigerator, she said. "Either of these options allow for gas exchange, unlike a plastic bag or plastic wrap, which will encourage bacterial growth and spoilage." Instead of dehydrating chanterelles, she recommends sautéing and freezing them. "However, I have seen folks who swear by dehydrated and ground chanterelle powder for cooking, so again there is some personal preference here."

Mushrooms are much in the news now with books such as Merlin Sheldrake's *Entangled Life: How Fungi Make Our Worlds, Change Our Minds, and Shape Our Futures* and Peter Wohlleben's *The Hidden Life of Trees*. The much-used term "the wood-wide web," which describes how mushrooms communicate with trees through the mycelium, has been attributed to Suzanne Simard's work described in her book *Finding the Mother Tree*. A great film about mushrooms is *Fantastic Fungi*. Still, despite all the interest in mushrooms, Swenie said that only 3 to 8 percent of the fungi in the world is currently described. "There are very few mycologists relative to other types of disciplines. Very few people take up that challenge. It's a wide-open field." Even amateurs have found new species. "There's a lot of opportunity," she said.

I asked Swenie for the definitive book on chanterelles and she said one doesn't exist. "The science has been changing so much that the literature hasn't kept up." But she and some fellow mycologists are working on a book about the mushrooms of the southern Appalachians. When it's published, I'll buy it.

Then I will be utterly positive about my mushroom identification.

CANTHARELLUS CIBARIUS MUSHROOM EPS10

Wild Apples

Goddesses are fabled to have contended for it, dragons were set to watch it, and heroes were employed to pluck it. . . . Surely the apple is the noblest of fruits.

—Henry David Thoreau in "Wild Apples"

A summer apple tree in the front yard is a wondrous thing.

I can sit on the front porch and watch apples fall to the ground, listen to the "plunk" as they hit the grass, and wildlife comes right to me. A squirrel climbs the tree, plucks an apple from a branch, and runs away with fruit in its mouth. Downy woodpeckers hang upside to peck on apples. Young bucks with velvet antlers sneak in to eat apples on the lawn and a groundhog waddles across the

grass, stands on his hind legs, and nibbles. Bold is he in the middle of the day with me watching—and two groundhog-chasing dogs.

Yellow jackets and ants finish off the bruised and half-eaten fruit. I got a painful sting once that itched for days afterward—simply trying to collect some fruit to make applesauce for the humans who dwell here.

In spring, I can stand underneath the apple tree and listen to the bees as they feast on the pink blossoms.

Ours are old apple trees, on the farm when we moved here. The tree closest to the porch, the one I watch so closely, already had cement in its center to support its trunk. The bark is ringed with woodpecker holes and a dead limb at the top is perfect for bird watching. It's amazing the tree still stands, no less produces a healthy supply of fruit—as long as we don't get a late spring frost. Its apples are small and yellow with white flesh, not perfectly round, full of scabs, certainly not fit for modern grocery store shelves. The tree is unusual because it fruits in July.

"Oh, you have a July apple," said a friend who grew up nearby. "It makes the best sauce." When she said that to me, I'd never heard the term *July apple* before—and she was correct, the applesauce is delicious.

How old is that apple tree, I've long wondered? What kind is it? Is it wild or grafted? Who planted it? Probably not Johnny Appleseed (aka John Chapman) though he did spread his seeds near this western Pennsylvania farm around 1800. Might our tree have been growing in 1862 when Thoreau lamented in his essay "Wild Apples" that the era of the wild apple will soon be past? "I see nobody planting trees to-day in such out-of-the way places, along the lonely roads and lanes, and at the bottom of dells in the woods."

When Thoreau wrote that essay, we had about fifteen thousand varieties of apples in this country, believed to have come from Kazakhstan via the Silk Road. (Only crabapples are native to our shores and they were called "spitters" because they tasted so bad one wanted to spit them out as soon as possible. "Spitters" were made into hard cider.) Apples received a name only if they were grown from seed and tasted good enough to eat fresh and pass on to neighbors and friends, said David Benscoter, who runs the Lost Apple Project in Washington state, where he's trying to save old apple varieties on the West Coast.

"Apples were incredibly important for homesteading families," he said. "A family might plant as many as one hundred apple trees to dry, make sauce, to can, for cider, and to make apple butter. Apples you could eat fresh from October until April or May were the most valuable of all."

After the Civil War, commercial growers decided apples had to be big, red, and uniform, and the varieties dwindled to about five thousand. From 1881 to 1945, according to the National Park Service, apple trees got smaller—from five feet tall to less than three—and went from a natural state to pruned. "The development of Red Delicious during this period had an enormous impact on apple growing, resulting in greater profitability for the industry, great fashionability of red apples, greater ubiquity of a single variety, and further obsolescence of superseded varieties," the NPS website states. By the 1940s, red delicious was the most common apple.

"Everyone shares a little of the blame for losing these apples," Benscoter said. "People bought apples with their eyes and only varieties with which they were familiar, like Red and Gold Delicious, Jonathan, and Mcintosh."

John Bunker, an apple historian who founded the Maine Heritage Orchard, is trying to save old apple varieties too—in Maine, New England, and New York. He believes different genetic combinations may fight apple diseases and pests and help trees deal with climate change. He thinks old apples are simply magical. "Apple trees are important in about fifty different ways," he said. "These old varieties connect people to history, place, families, and their own past." He believes they're emblematic of a whole culture, teach us about the ground we live on, and unlock mysteries of who came before us. They might be the key to breeding the apples of our future, he said.

I was hoping our craggy old tree might be one of those keys.

Bunker said many apple varieties are still left yet to be rediscovered in places like our lawns, but time is of the essence. "The apples planted by the old settlers could live one hundred to one hundred and fifty, maybe two hundred years. The last of those old trees are now coming to the end of their natural lives and are dying rapidly. The time is right now to find the last lost apples."

Benscoter agreed. "We need to find them before we die."

Apples are difficult to propagate. One can't just plant a seed into soil and expect to get the same tree. That's because apples are heterozygotes, meaning that "an apple tree from seed will not be a tree like its parent, but will resemble a more distant ancestor." That definition is courtesy of my great-grandfather, Charles Burkett, who wrote a book in 1903 (with Stevens and Hill) called *Agriculture for Beginners*. The only way to faithfully reproduce an apple is by grafting—and grafting has changed over the years. Trees grafted onto modern dwarfing rootstocks don't live as long as the old trees, Bunker said, only thirty to forty years.

I figured my questions about our old apple tree were unusual, but Bunker said no, such questions are being asked by countless people across New England who send him apples to date and identify. I did the same—twelve apples individually wrapped in newspaper, information about when our town was settled, photos of the tree and its bark, and a photo of the tree from 1941 (I know at the very least it was here then). I sent apples to Benscoter too, who passed them on to Shaun Shepherd and Joanie Cooper at the Temperate Orchard Conservancy in Oregon.

To determine what sort of apple we have, the two teams looked at fruit shape and skin color, and over a dozen other distinguishing characteristics, including the stem, calyx, core, sepals, seeds, and stamen. "Identifying apples can be pretty picky work," Bunker said.

Bunker knew of no cultivar called a "July apple," a local nickname he surmised, and said he rarely sees summer apples at all. "If one had fifty trees, only one to two would have been summer apples." He confirmed that summer apples were generally planted next to houses, because they don't store well and if not watched carefully and picked right away, they'd rot or get eaten by wildlife.

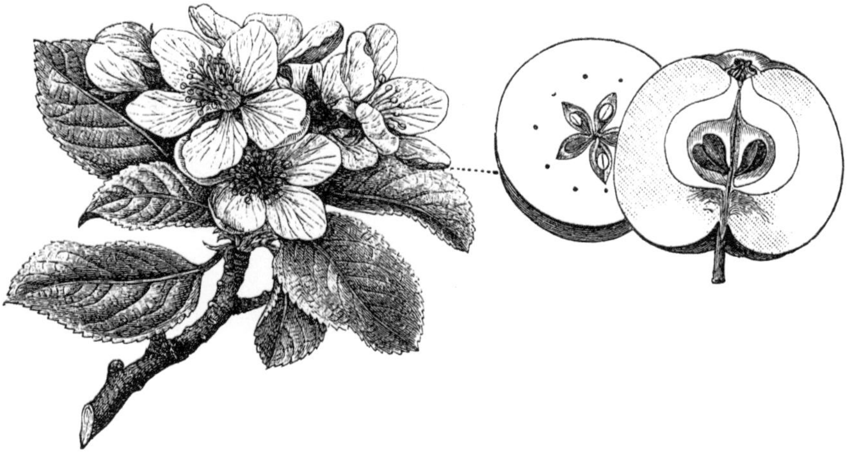

In the end, I got two slightly different opinions. Bunker believes our apple tree "most closely resembles" an "Early Harvest," 130–150 years old, a fairly common variety of summer apple in 1850. "High quality summer-ripening apples were uncommon overall, and when a good one came along—like 'Early Harvest'—they were coveted," he said. "Now, 170 years later, it is extremely rare, definitely an heirloom."

Benscoter's team identified our tree as "Early Ripe," which likely came from a seed on a farm in Adams County, Pennsylvania, circa 1800, a rare apple first recorded in 1867, but not extinct. The two varieties are similar and apparently easily confused.

Bunker concluded that our tree is grafted, which surprised me as I see no evidence of grafting. "The graft on old trees is sometimes quite obvious," he said, "and sometimes not visible at all."

I may not save the planet with this old tree, but I'm happy to have narrowed the variety down to two. And I'm pleased to know about how long the tree has been here. I still don't know if it was planted by the original settler who built this log house around 1860, but I'm guessing it was. And knowing this makes me feel closer to those who walked this ground before me.

Since apple trees can take four to ten years to bear fruit, Bunker said whoever planted the tree sent us a gift. "The people who planted that tree may never have eaten that apple," he said. "Old apples are a gift from people long ago, saying to us: 'This is for you.'"

A gift, indeed—for those of us currently renting this speck of earth—and for the wildlife with whom we share it.

Carpenter Bees

We raised our babies in this old farmhouse, wrapped them in swaddling clothes like little cocoons, protected them as best as we could. We renovated parts of the house, added a bathroom, and knocked through a kitchen wall to create more space for a growing family. We fed our children, taught them what we knew. We sent them out into the world.

That's all carpenter bees want to do.

The female uses her powerful mandibles to chew nearly perfectly round half-inch holes into our front porch railings. She bores an inch deep, then turns at right angles along the wood grain to create tunnels with individual chambers where she lays her eggs. Each baby gets its own bedroom. To nourish them as they transform from egg to larva, pupae to adult, she leaves behind "bee bread," a mixture of pollen and nectar. She plugs the holes with sawdust and wood pulp and departs.

She works so hard that if she has to build her own birthing rooms, she can have four to five babies; if she inherits an existing nest, she can have twelve or more. She chews with such force that her mandibles wear out. She gathers so much food for her young that her wings get tattered and she can no longer fly. Sometimes she has help from a subordinate queen who's waiting for her to die to take over the real estate. She lives only one season.

If I look up *carpenter bees*, I'm offered a host of exterminators, "professional bee removal teams" that claim the females have painful stings that can cause life-threatening allergic reactions. That carpenter bees are a serious property threat—males frighten people and bee feces stain surfaces. Dangerous predators, they say, are sure to follow carpenter bees. The companies promote insecticide.

But I don't want to use insecticide. I don't want to kill the carpenter bees. I just want to protect our porch railing.

I try less harmful remedies. I surround the porch with bee motels and cavity-nesting bees move in—but not carpenter bees. I spray lemon oil into the holes—citrus and almond oils are said to deter them—but that does nothing. Websites suggest offering them brush piles and snags as alternatives—well, we certainly have no shortage of those on the farm—and still, the carpenter bees prefer our porch. They're said to dislike painted surfaces and our porch is

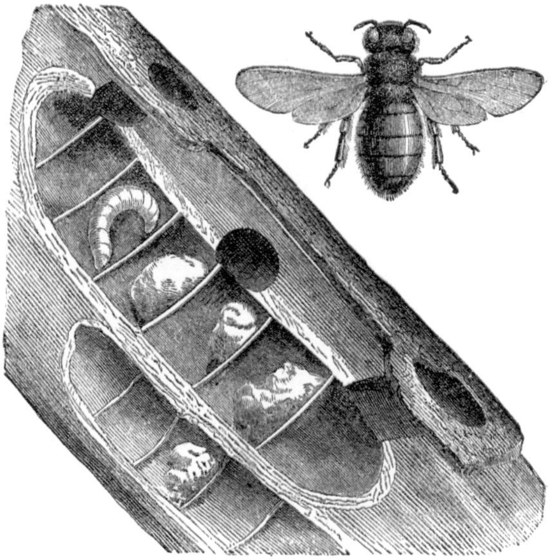

CARPENTER BEE

painted white—but if I contort myself and turn upside down to look underneath the railing, I see unpainted access holes, impossible to paint without removing the railing. Wind chimes are said to discourage them, but I'd rather listen to the sound of the buzzing bees. I do not try fake wasp nests.

What's a homeowner to do?

"There is a narrative that these bees are destructive and dangerous and it simply isn't true in most cases," said Kate Anton, lab manager for the Grozinger Lab at Penn State's Center for Pollinator Research. Severe infestations can jeopardize buildings, she said, but that generally happens to untreated surfaces and when woodpeckers decide to eat the carpenter bees. "A few carpenter bees are not going to threaten a structure," she said. And she doesn't think I'll ever lure them elsewhere. "I don't know anything that is successful in persuading them away," she said.

The eastern carpenter bee (*Xylocopa virginica*; *Xylocopa* means wood cutter) is native to Pennsylvania and important to our ecosystem for many reasons. It provides food for birds, decomposes fallen trees, and puts nutrients back into the soil. "Eighty percent of flowering plants depend on bees for pollination," Anton said, and carpenter bees are good pollinators. They use what's called "buzz pollination," which is when a bee grasps a flower with its jaw, vibrates its wings, and releases huge amounts of pollen, particularly useful for pollinating blueberries, tomatoes, eggplant, and peppers. They—and bumblebee queens—are our largest native bees, so they can fly when smaller bees are grounded and they pollinate later into autumn than other bees. (It's easy to confuse carpenter bees with bumblebees. Bumblebees have fuzzy abdomens that are black and gold, whereas the carpenter bee abdomen is shiny and all black.)

For ten summers, maybe longer, I've observed the female carpenter bee climb in and out of her borings. I've seen undeveloped babies fall out of the porch railing, perhaps awakened too soon from hibernation. I've seen four-toothed mason wasps take over carpenter bee nests and deliver carpenter bee caterpillars to their own young. I've watched piles of sawdust called "frass" accumulate on the porch floor and I've been dive-bombed by the male carpenter bee as I walk in and out of the front door. His buzz is loud and he gets so close to my face that I can see the white square on his. But he amuses me because I know he's only doing what a carpenter bee father does—defend his territory and protect his babies—and I know he cannot sting. (Females do, but rarely, because they have too much work to do.)

Our human structures are one reason the carpenter bee population is stable. We give them more places to nest. By contrast, our bumblebees, which

generally nest underground, are in trouble. Of Pennsylvania's eighteen species, five are of conservation concern and one, the rusty patched bumblebee, is endangered, having lost 90 percent of its range. Carpenter bees are also stable because they forage on a wide diversity of plants, Anton said. "While some species of bees require very precise plants and environments, the sturdy carpenter bee can make do in our changing climate."

For people who want to eliminate carpenter bees, some websites suggest sealing holes with steel wool or copper gauze, dowel rods and wood putty, but Anton says they'll get out. "You can entomb them but they will chew themselves a new exit," she said. Other websites suggest inserting wire deep into the holes and skewering them. But Anton said the only way to get rid of them is to dust the nest with pyrethrum, which she suggests only if the structure is at serious risk.

"This pesticide is toxic to cats and insects and certainly it is not something that anyone would want on their skin," she said. Use a professional, she advised. "I would urge everyone to first evaluate the risk of the bees and compare that to the risk of pesticide exposure."

Anton thinks if I've had carpenter bees for ten years and my porch is still intact that I may not have cause for worry. We don't know for sure, of course, but nevertheless, I'm going to leave my bees alone. Others may think differently, may be driven crazy with annoyance or worry, but I think it's at least worth considering how these amazing bees contribute to our very existence. If we understand better the lives of the creatures that surround us—how in many ways they may be similar to us—we might think twice before grabbing the insecticide. For me, it's a wonder to be this close to nature, and besides, having given birth to two children, I've aligned myself with that mama carpenter bee—with her worn-out mandibles and her tattered wings.

Purslane

Henry David Thoreau gathered purslane in a cornfield. He boiled and salted it and called it "a satisfactory dinner." When writing about the plant in *Walden*, he made sure to include its Latin name—*Portulaca oleracea*—"on account of the savoriness of the trivial name." By trivial name, I assume he's referring to purslane's common names: *little hogweed* and *pigweed*. Perhaps he found the Latin nomenclature more appetizing?

"I learned from my two years' experience," Thoreau went on to write, "that it would cost incredibly little trouble to obtain one's necessary food, even in this latitude, that a man may use as simple a diet as the animals, and yet retain health and strength."

I eat purslane's succulent, green leaves raw with olive oil, lemon—and a dash of salt. Often while working in the vegetable garden, I snip off a piece and eat it there. The leaves, stems, yellow flowers, and seeds are edible and the herb can be eaten in many ways, such as a garnish on sandwiches, stir-fried, pickled, braised, as a pesto, or in soups (the plant contains a thickening agent). I could make satisfactory meals all summer long as it grows wild in my flower and vegetable gardens and in the pavement at the edge of the driveway. I saw it last August in front of a local pharmacy.

Yet I daresay most people don't even notice it—and if they do, they think it a weed and yank it out. I bet they don't know its name. And that's a shame because purslane is a gift from nature, free of charge, and incredibly healthy.

"A superfood," said Calyx Liddick, an ethnobotanist at the Northern Appalachian School in Harrisburg. She has purslane in her patio and the cracks of her city sidewalks.

One of the distinguishing features of this ancient plant is that it is exceptionally high in omega-3 fatty acids—some sources say the highest amount of any vegetable and five times the amount in spinach. It contains vitamins such as A, C, and E and small amounts of B vitamins, Liddick said, which most plants do not. It has minerals, including potassium, magnesium, calcium,

and iron, and is high in antioxidants like beta-carotene, glutathione, melatonin, and betalain.

"It is a good example of the overlap of food and medicine," Liddick said. "The line between food and medicine is often blurred and purslane feels like a food that can be used as a medicine."

And lest you think only foragers and ethnobotanists rave about purslane, read what our National Institutes of Health (NIH) says about the plant: "The antioxidant content and nutritional value of purslane are important for human consumption. It revealed tremendous nutritional potential and has indicated the potential use of this herb for the future."

The plant is used to treat insect bites, wounds and bleeding, digestive disorders such as gastric ulcers, and modulates inflammation, Liddick said. It has been studied as an anticancer agent and as an aid to reduce heart disease. The Chinese treat diabetes with purslane and call it "a vegetable for long life." Native Americans use it for earaches and worms, among other remedies. It's commonly eaten in France, where it has the alliterative name of *pourpier potager*.

In Mexico, the herb is called *verdolagas* and has been used in traditional cooking for many years. The Tarahumara tribe grind the seeds into flour. I told my Spanish teacher, who is Mexican, about the abundance of it growing in my vegetable garden and she was thrilled. I gave her a basket full and she made me a delicious stew: *puerco en salsa verde con verdolagas* (purslane in green sauce with pork, but she substituted chicken).

No one seems to know exactly where purslane originated—guesses include North Africa, Asia, and South America—but the plant now grows around the world in a wide range of soil. A hardy plant, it can withstand drought and even some pollution; it reproduces from broken stems and by thousands of tiny black seeds.

Liddick ranked purslane high on a list of the healthiest wild edible plants, along with stinging nettles and lamb's quarters. "It's underrated because people think it is just a weed," she said, "but it is almost like taking a daily vitamin." She loves wild foods because they are more nutritionally dense than what we can get at the grocery store, even if we are buying top quality produce, she said. And in gardens, people pull out wild plants only to replace them with

less-dense nutrient versions. "They pull out lamb's quarters to plant its cousin, domesticated spinach. That pales in comparison. If we know how to manage edible weeds, we can leave them and have more food!"

I managed the herb, which grew abundantly in my vegetable garden last summer, not only by eating it, but by leaving it as a ground cover. Why pull it out? Purslane grew underneath a trellis where I'd planted climbing baby butternut squash and beneath my tomato plants. I left it as living mulch.

"We need an awareness and a cultural shift," Liddick said. "There are all these little plants that we ignore. Why? Because you can't find them in the grocery store. But you can find them in your yard!" Of course, you have to know how to identify them, she said, but this is a skill that anyone can learn.

Purslane's main contraindication, Liddick said, is that it is high in oxalic acid, as are rhubarb and spinach. That might give you a stomachache or encourage kidney stones if you eat it in large quantities, so be careful if you are prone to that, she said.

Purslane can also be confused with spotted spurge, which is toxic. The plants resemble each other somewhat and often grow in the same place. Spurge, however, has a flat, nonsucculent leaf and emits a milky substance if a stem is broken. Spurge also has hairy leaves, which purslane does not. Purslane's flowers are yellow and spurge's pink.

So stop for a minute. Take a look at the ground for a mounding plant, with fleshy, cactus-like leaves and reddish tendrils that sprawl in all directions. I suspect that once you identify purslane, you'll see it everywhere. Cut off a stem and have a bite. Experiment a little. Try it with mozzarella and tomato, in a Turkish soup or a version of Argentine chimichurri.

Who said there's no free lunch?

One Lone Bat

"THINGS REVEAL THEMSELVES PASSING AWAY," WENDELL BERRY WROTE.

I never noticed so many ash trees in the forest until the emerald ash borer began to kill them. The drumming of the ruffed grouse is dearer to me now because of its absence. But of all the things on the farm that have revealed themselves by passing away, none is more striking than our bats. Thirty-five years ago, scores of bats zipped around our skies at dusk, but last summer as I walked across the lawn to close the chicken coop every night, I saw one lone bat.

I used to sweep up bat guano when cleaning horse stalls and collect bat guano from upstairs in the barn to use as fertilizer on the garden. Piles of bat guano once accumulated below two window shutters on the house where bats hung upside down by their toes during the day. But no longer. One lone bat flew into our bedroom last summer, but that used to be commonplace in this drafty old farmhouse.

Pennsylvania's northern long-eared bat was just reclassified as endangered, meaning that the species is at a "very high" risk of extinction. It joins another endangered Pennsylvania bat—the Indiana bat. Since we have only six hibernating bat species, that's a third of our hibernating bats. (Pennsylvania also has three migratory bats.) Pennsylvania's little brown bat may be next.

"We have 1 percent of the population we used to have here," said Mollie Byrne, a Wildlife Disease Biology Technician at the Pennsylvania Game Commission. "It's hard to wrap your brain around a decline that substantial."

The decline is caused largely by humans: habitat destruction, pesticides, pollution, too much light at night, highway deaths, slaughter, and wind farms. "So many things we do as a society are detrimental to bats," Byrne said. But worst of all is a fungal disease called white-nose syndrome, brought to the US by spelunkers who visited European caves. The disease was discovered in 2006 in New York state and now affects bats in thirty-eight states and eight Canadian provinces. The fungus attacks bats' noses, ears, and wing membranes and turns their noses—if not their entire bodies—white. They fidget and rub their faces, which awakens them from hibernation, then they fly around using energy they've stored to survive winter and starve to death.

Until white-nose syndrome appeared, bats had been with us for fifty million years. They're the second largest order of mammals after rodents and the only mammal that can fly. Fourteen hundred species exist across the world, on every continent except Antarctica, and they are crucial to our planet as pollinators, seed dispensers, and insectivores. But bats are so mired in myth and superstition that despite their gigantic drop in numbers, people don't rally around them as they do elephants, pandas, or whales. Many people believe bats suck your blood (Pennsylvania has no vampire bats), are dirty (bats groom themselves like

housecats), carry rabies (they do, but transmission to humans is rare), and that bat guano contains tuberculosis (there is no evidence of this).

Bats don't fly into your hair either, though I admit I've been spooked by bats swooping up and down in the house, thinking perhaps they *are* aiming for my hair. Byrne explained to me why bats fly this way. "They're insanely curious," she said. "If you put up a basketball net, they'll fly around it all night trying to figure it out. They want to know what you are too. They mean no harm. They know you're a lot bigger than they are."

Still, why should we care if bats go extinct?

We should care because bats eat insects, and a lot of them—moths, June bugs, flies, leafhoppers, and mosquitos—up to a million a year. A single bat can eat one-quarter of its weight in one meal and 4,500 mosquitos in one night, which helps protect us from mosquito-borne diseases such as malaria, Zika, and West Nile. (For the record, West Nile has contributed to the decline of the ruffed grouse.)

Bats are "a keystone species," which means they play a key role in our ecosystem and if we lose them, our food web will crash. Estimates are that bats save farmers $5 billion a year in crop damage due to common agricultural pests such as the cucumber beetle—and without bats to combat these pests, farmers may resort to using pesticides and insecticides, which aren't good for our health, or the planet's. "Bats are an amazing natural defense, but that is disappearing," Byrne said.

As a gardener, I care, because with fewer big brown bats—Pennsylvania's most common bat—my cucumber vines were decimated last summer by cucumber beetles, nighttime feeders that eat pumpkins, squash, eggplant, tomatoes, and melons. Cucumber beetles also caused bacterial wilt on geraniums and poppies in my flower garden and their larva is a pest called corn rootworm. If your house is overrun by the invasive marmorated stink bug, you might care because big brown bats eat stink bugs too.

Pennsylvania's bats hibernate largely in natural caves and abandoned limestone mines—called hibernacula—most of which are already contaminated by the white-nose syndrome. The Pennsylvania Game Commission has tried for seventeen years to eradicate the fungus, but their goal now, Byrne said, "is to get individual bats to survive long enough to reproduce." That's a challenge even in the best of times as Pennsylvania's bats reproduce slowly—giving birth once a year to one pup only, blind and naked at birth, which have only a 50 percent chance of survival.

The Game Commission is also gating caves so bats cannot be disturbed during hibernation and adding what are called "cold air sinks" to make mines colder—forty to forty-five degrees—because the fungus performs best at fifty-three degrees. As bats depart in spring, fungicide is being sprayed in "every possible nook and cranny," Byrne said, "to kill off the fungus before bats return in the fall."

We can help too—by staying out of hibernacula, hanging bat boxes, planting native plants, and removing bats gently from our homes. "The biggest thing homeowners can do if they end up with a bat in the house," Byrne said, "is please don't kill it. Call a professional if you can't get it outside yourself."

And we can change the narrative. Instead of looking at bats as Dracula, we might consider them cute and curious little mammals simply trying to figure out their universe. After all, aren't we just big mammals trying to figure out ours?

An Avian Murder Case on a Quiet Back Porch

I OPEN THE PANTRY DOOR AND THE EASTERN PHOEBE FLIES OFF THE NEST. Her cup-shaped home is made of mud, covered in moss and cantilevered over a glass light fixture—an avian Fallingwater. Her nest placement makes sense because before eastern phoebes lived so close to humans, they built their nests on cliffs. Every year for thirty-five years we've had an eastern phoebe nest under the eaves of our back porch. Without her it would not be spring.

Eastern phoebes are in the flycatcher family and consume not just flies, but also wasps, grasshoppers, and even ticks—great news to those of us who can't walk in the woods without bringing home the scourge. Native to North America, eastern phoebes also eat small berries from our native plants such as Virginia creeper. Its call is like its name: an onomatopoeic "fee bee."

I puzzled at first if the bird might be an eastern wood-pewee, another grayish white flycatcher with a short bill, but the giveaway was the way the eastern phoebe wags her tail when she flies off the nest and lands on the lilac bush by the stream.

Eastern phoebes have the distinction of being the first bird ever banded—in 1804 by John James Audubon himself. He, too, watched an eastern phoebe nest at his farm in Mill Grove, Pennsylvania, about two hundred miles directly east of here as the flycatcher flies. One autumn day, the story goes, he tied silver threads onto the legs of five nestlings before they migrated south and reported that two of the marked birds returned the next spring.

On our farm, eastern phoebes are among the first birds to return from the southern United States or Mexico, and the female at my backdoor was sitting on her first clutch of eggs by mid-April. Females lay two to six white eggs, maybe with dots of red and brown, and usually two clutches a year. Every day I watch her from my perch—a kitchen table that doubles as a desk.

But this year I'm worried. One day last spring when I went to check on her, I found raw and naked eastern phoebe nestlings tossed onto the porch floor. At first, I suspected brown-headed cowbirds, famous as they are for raiding nests. But I'd observed house sparrows dive-bombing the back door, which I'd never seen before, and then learned that while brown-headed cowbirds often remove eggs to make room for their own, they don't dump out nestlings.

Which meant a nonnative bird was killing our native birds. House sparrows, originally from Europe and Asia, were brought to Brooklyn in the 1850s to control caterpillars. By 1870, their introduction had incited a "Sparrow War" between two ornithologists who disagreed on whether it was a good idea. Though house sparrow numbers in the United States are down—to eighty million today from four hundred million in 1966—they are still one of our most common birds, and we've had an explosion of them on the farm. They nest in gutters and hanging lanterns and are aggressive when competing for nesting space.

According to the Cornell Lab of Ornithology, house sparrows have been known to attack many bird species, including bluebirds, purple martins, and tree swallows. The situation is so bad for eastern bluebirds that the North American Bluebird Society recommends removing and destroying house sparrow eggs from bluebird boxes and trapping adult house sparrows. (Be sure house sparrows are the culprits, they advise, because native species are strictly protected under the Migratory Bird Treaty Act.)

Kill house sparrows? Smash their eggs? Isn't there anything less lethal I can do in my own sparrow war?

"Yes, there is," says Robert Mulvihill, an ornithologist at the National Aviary in Pittsburgh. "I know my position is at odds with some of my colleagues, but I don't blame the house sparrow," he says. "Introduced or not, they are now a fully naturalized wild North American species and I don't think any wild bird should be labeled the bad guy just for doing what it naturally does to survive."

Mulvihill said he was surprised that a century and a half of nest competition hadn't resulted in more defensive behavior in bluebirds. They just need to adapt, he said, and we can help bluebirds by putting bluebird boxes only where they belong: not near houses, barns, or bird feeders but in open meadows, where house sparrows would never call home.

"Eastern phoebes have to regroup and find safer nesting sites," Mulvihill said, "preferably forested settings near streams, where they breed naturally."

Eastern phoebes are an early nesting species and may have traditionally had their first brood before competition from later-nesting house sparrows, he explained. "But warmer spring weather induces house sparrows to nest earlier in some areas, and eastern phoebes may have lost their usual seasonal head start," he says.

To Mulvihill, killing house sparrows is an all-too-typical human response. "Let's be honest," he said. "If bluebirds and eastern phoebes have an enemy, it is we humans, not the house sparrows we brought here."

First, Mulvihill pointed out, we wanted the sparrows to control pest insects. "They did that, and made themselves at home," he said. "Now we don't want them because they are too good at competing with other birds we want around. This is a lesson why you never want to introduce an adaptable species into a new environment because it will inevitably upset the ecological balance and create problems."

"It rarely ends well," Mulvihill added.

This human may be part of the problem too. I could stop feeding the birds by February, which might cause year-round residents like house sparrows to disperse. I could avoid inexpensive bird food mixes that contain cracked corn, milo, wheat, and rye, preferred by house sparrows, and use more expensive seed that contains black oil sunflower seeds, safflower seeds, and white millet. I

could change from a platform feeder to a tubular one that house sparrows can't dominate as easily.

Still, as the climate changes and species relocate, we may all have to get used to seeing birds compete for nesting space in our own backyards. The problem, Mulvihill predicted, is "going to snowball."

I've broken up rooster fights, but it seems there's little I can do on a large scale about competition between wild birds. Even if you tried to kill all the house sparrows at your house, Mulvihill said, "you'd be doing that year in and year out."

Still, I'm on the lookout this spring for nest-raiding house sparrows. I will watch whatever scene plays out at my own back door, witnessing the results of human interaction in the bird world: a mother bird simply trying to raise her young, dealing as best she can with what we humans have thrown at her.

The Indian Pipe

An eerie plant appears in the woods. I bend down and study its translucent white color, ghostly against the vibrant green of midsummer. The three-inch stems have specks of gray and black and its tiny leaves resemble scales. Some of the pipe-shaped flowers stand upright, while others droop in a melancholy manner.

I think it might be a fungus of some sort. But, I am wrong.

The Indian pipe (*Monotropa uniflora*) is a Pennsylvania wildflower. It is also called ghost pipe, corpse plant, and ice plant.

I learn that Indian pipe was a special flower to Emily Dickinson, perhaps her favorite. She included it in her herbarium and a drawing of it appeared on the front cover of her first book of poems. That drawing was sent to her by Mabel Loomis Todd, a woman Dickinson never met in person and who didn't know that Indian pipe was so important to Dickinson. Dickinson wrote to thank the artist: "That without suspecting it you should send me the preferred flower of life, seems almost supernatural, and the sweet glee that I felt at meeting it I could confide to none. I still cherish the clutch with which I bore it from the ground when a wondering Child, an unearthly booty and maturity only enhances mystery, never decreases it."

Of all the exquisite flowers in the world, Indian pipe was one of Dickinson's favorites? What might this tell us about the reclusive poet? Marta McDowell, author of *Emily Dickinson's Gardens*, has a theory: "Emily was like Indian Pipes," she writes. "She relied on family members . . . for major exchanges with the outside world: necessities, protection and news."

The Indian pipe cannot live without the help of others either—specifically other plants. It has no chlorophyll and cannot photosynthesize, so to survive it depends on a milky cap mushroom in the *Russulaceae* family. That mushroom, through its symbiotic mycorrhizal connection with other plants, exchanges nutrients with host trees such as beech, pine, and oak and passes those nutrients back to the Indian pipe.

Dickinson wrote about the Indian pipe in a poem "drafted on a fragment of ruled stationery paper in 1879," according to the Morgan Library.

'Tis whiter than an Indian Pipe—
'Tis dimmer than a Lace—
No stature has it, like a Fog
When you approach the place—
Not any voice imply it here—
Or intimate it there—
A spirit—how doth it accost—
What function hath the Air?
This limitless Hyperbole
Each one of us shall be—
'Tis Drama—if Hypothesis
It be not Tragedy—

I ask Cristanne Miller to explain the poem to me. Miller is editor of *Emily Dickinson's Poems: As She Preserved Them* and coeditor of *The Letters of Emily Dickinson*. (For the record, Miller said Dickinson loved other flowers also, including violets, roses, jasmine, and even clovers.) The poem, she explained, functions like a riddle: *"What is 'it' that is 'whiter . . . dimmer,' hidden, and so on. In the last six lines it appears that this 'it' may be a spirit, a 'Hyperbole' representing what would probably be the inner life of 'each one of us.' We all have our own 'Drama' of life—and when we are lucky that drama is not a 'Tragedy.'"*

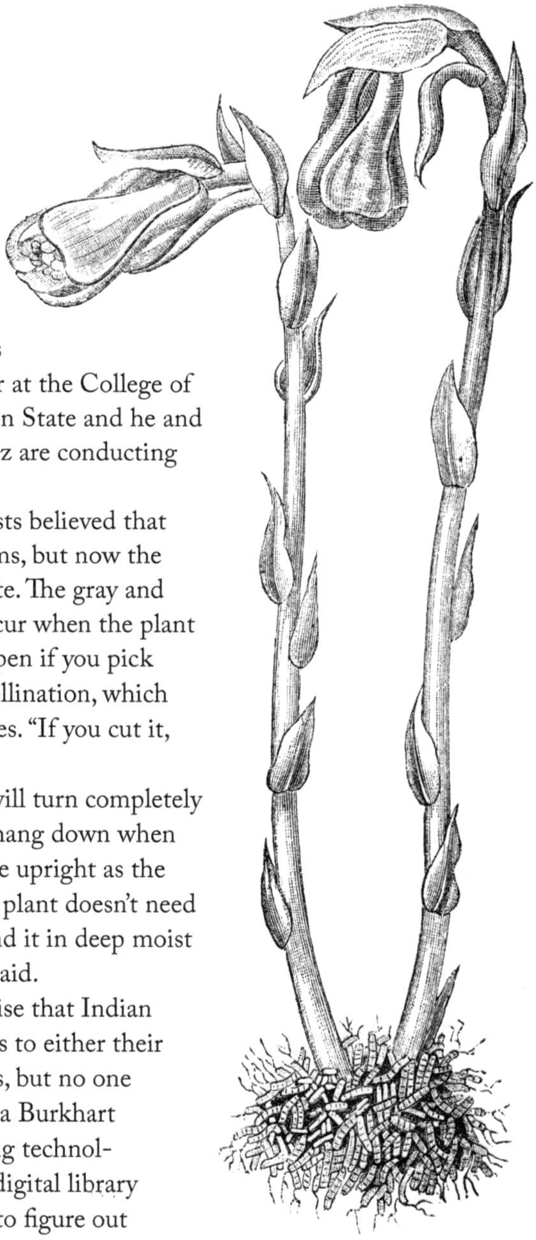

After seeing Indian pipes for the first time, people always ask Eric Burkhart, "What kind of mushroom is this?" Burkhart is a professor at the College of Agricultural Sciences at Penn State and he and PhD student Savannah Anez are conducting research on the plant.

For years, he said, scientists believed that Indian pipes were mushrooms, but now the plant is classified as a parasite. The gray and black specks, he told me, occur when the plant gets bruised, which can happen if you pick the plant and also during pollination, which is largely done by bumblebees. "If you cut it, within twelve to twenty-four hours the white plant will turn completely black," he said. The flowers hang down when they first emerge but become upright as the flower matures. Because the plant doesn't need sunlight at all, "you often find it in deep moist hemlock stands," Burkhart said.

Scientists currently surmise that Indian pipes do not return nutrients to either their mushroom hosts or the trees, but no one is positive and that's one area Burkhart and Anez are studying. Using technology called metabolomics, a digital library of molecules, they're trying to figure out exactly which molecules the plant contains. They're also studying the plant's medicinal uses.

Indian pipe was long thought to be poisonous, although Native Americans have used it as an eyewash and an anticonvulsant. In the last twenty years, however, the plant has become popular on the Internet as a pain-relieving agent and as relief from psychological trauma, Burkhart said.

In 1889, a single study looked for what are called grayanotoxins in Indian pipes, which led to the conclusion that the plant was toxic. But the Penn State team did their own study recently, the results of which were published in the *Journal of Natural Products*. "It was the most thorough study ever done on grayanotoxins," Burkhart said. "We strongly suspect there are no grayanotoxins at this point."

Burkhart and Anez seek to answer this question: "Do current folk uses, especially for pain management, have any phytochemical explanations?"

I rejoice in what I have growing on this farm, in my own backyard. That it exists here at all, that I was lucky enough to find it, and that I was able to discover such interesting facts about the plant—both literary and scientific. I only wish I could know what a famous nineteenth-century, nature-loving poet might have thought about other people's fascination with Indian pipes and the potential medicinal properties of her mysterious "preferred flower of life."

ENVIRONMENT

What a Search for the Signs of Spring Reveals

If you looked into the sky before dawn on Monday, you may have seen the worm moon.

That's the name some Native Americans give the March full moon because that's when the soil warms and earthworms emerge. Others call it crust moon, when snow melts and refreezes, and sap moon, when maple trees are tapped.

But we've had little snow to melt because this winter was the warmest on record for the lower forty-eight states, and my friends tapped their trees in February. All of this makes me wonder: Which signs of spring still align with such ancient wisdom?

I've been thinking about that on my walks around our Pennsylvania farm.

Few finer places exist to observe the onset of spring than a pond. The spotted salamander has already attached her white, globular egg masses to forsythia branches that dip below the water's surface and wood frogs, with their little black Zorro masks, leap off the bank in front of me into the deep.

Henry David Thoreau called wood frogs "the very voice of the weather," and what a voice it is: a deep, repetitive croak like the strumming of a banjo. Wood frogs basically freeze during winter and are one of the first frogs to emerge from leaf litter and breed in spring, which is when the females lay masses of gelatinous, black-speckled eggs on the pond's edge.

But my favorite frog is the spring peeper, whose mating call surrounds our sleeping porch at night with a sound so loud and high-pitched I could swear spaceships are landing. Who can't love a one-inch, nocturnal, camouflaged tree frog with an X on its back? All amphibians are threatened by wetland destruction, but spring peepers are widespread here.

By the creek, skunk cabbage pokes up reliably from the muck, its speckled, maroon-yellow spathe resembling a jester's cap. I get down on my hands and knees and sniff its scent, likened to rotten meat, which pollinators apparently adore, and I inadvertently scare away a fly hovering around the spiky, prehistoric-looking flower called a spadix.

Skunk cabbage fascinates me because it's one of a small group of plants that can generate its own heat. It could even melt the snow around it, if we had any. It's an ancient plant, with us since dinosaurs roamed the earth, but it is now endangered in Tennessee. Can Pennsylvania's skunk cabbage be far behind?

Near a path in the woods, I see my first spring beauty. As the weather warms, I'll be on the lookout for our other native wildflowers, like Virginia bluebells, trillium, and trout lily. Spring ephemerals, they're called. Their name alone is magical! These flowers sprout when sunlight streams onto the forest floor, before the trees leaf out. But they don't stay with us long, having only a brief window in which to bloom and be pollinated. Then, they die back completely, as if they were never here. I worry, though. We have so many deer eating them, and invasive plants are taking over their territory.

In the old cow pasture, I hear what is dependably our first returning songbird: the red-winged blackbird, plentiful in North America. And at dawn from the apple tree outside my bedroom window, I hear the first "fee bee." That means the eastern phoebe is back and soon she'll

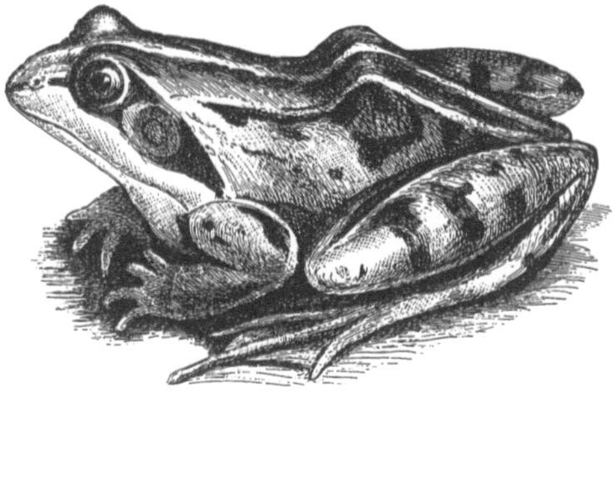

freshen up the nest on the light fixture at the pantry door that's been used every year for thirty-six years.

I await the chimney swifts. Not for their song, but for the funnel cloud they create at dusk as they fly round and round like fighter pilots trying to dive into our nineteenth-century stone chimney. Sometimes I rescue a baby that has fallen down into the hearth, the closest a human can get to a bird that spends all day on the wing. But where once we had many of these insectivores raising their young, last year we saw few. They've declined 70 percent over the past fifty years, researchers say, largely because of habitat loss and pesticides that kill the insects they rely on for food.

When I forage for ramps, also known as wild leeks, I do so sustainably. Someone took a dining-room-table-size portion of them out of the woods not long ago and irresponsible foragers sell masses of them to restaurants. This has caused the plant to be listed as vulnerable in many states.

I get lucky and find a patch of scarlet elf cup mushrooms, which grow on dead wood and whose name conjures up elves frolicking about the forest. Their color enchants me, too: an orange exterior and brilliant red interior that catches rainwater. Some say they're edible, though I haven't tried them.

I've long foraged for morels, which I do eat, sautéed in butter and piled deliciously on toast. Locals tell me, however, there aren't as many as there once were. The black morel fruits first, any day now, when the ground temperature reaches fifty degrees, according to lore. But May is when I find my prized specimens, golden and eight inches tall, if the stars align.

I like to imagine fairies having meetings atop the umbrella-like leaves of May apples. This native plant is poisonous except for the ripe, yellow fruit (discard the seeds, a forager-friend says) but people here make May apple jelly and wine. Small mammals eat the fruit, as do box turtles, important in dispersing the seeds.

May apples are used in wart medicine and are being studied as an anticancer agent. We have large colonies around

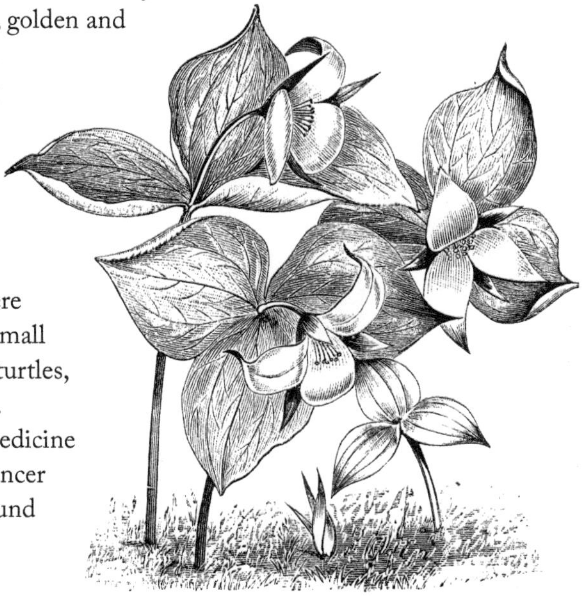

the farm, but the plant is in trouble in Vermont and Florida.

In the understory of a gray March wood, I see sparkles of yellow: the tiny, delicate flower clusters of spicebush. I snip some twigs to brew a spring tonic. This aromatic plant can substitute for allspice and is a host plant of the spicebush swallowtail butterfly. In fall, the wood thrush eats the red berries before migrating to the Gulf of Mexico.

We have no shortage of stinging nettles, which I eat raw, despite the burning of my fingers and tongue. Most people think of this plant as a weed and try to eradicate it, but it has amazing medicinal and culinary properties. I already have a rash on both wrists from poison ivy, a plant thriving in our warming climate, growing 70 percent faster with more carbon dioxide in the atmosphere.

In my wanderings through the fields and forests of this old farm, it's easy to forget what's happening to the plants and animals around me. It all looks so beautiful, so peaceful. But all I have to do is peel away a thin pastoral veneer to witness how many signs of spring are no longer in sync with the old rhythms of the season.

Still, I cannot help but rejoice in these, the harbingers of spring, and the rebirth they symbolize.

Plants die, but come back. Birds leave, but reappear. Frogs freeze and then sing their hearts out. Mushrooms fruit once more. Aren't we all just spring ephemerals anyway? Shining as gloriously as we are able and then gone?

And I am optimistic about one sign of spring we thought we'd lost: the budding, almost fluorescent green leaves of the ash tree. Hundreds of ash have toppled over in these woods because of the emerald ash borer. But some trees, it turns out, did not succumb to the brilliant green beetle. These survivors have become known as lingering ash, and from them scientists are breeding new trees. In certain areas there are also reports of an increase in ash seedlings and saplings.

Perhaps none of these will make it to maturity. No one knows yet. Not in my lifetime, certainly. But maybe, just maybe, our grandchildren's generation will be able to see a bright, spring moon rise above those towering ash trees once again.

What Would Rachel Carson Say?

On a Tuesday morning in August, I turned out of my driveway onto Route 711, a two-lane state road, a main north-south corridor designated as the Laurel Highlands Scenic Byway. I passed, heading in the other direction, two large white trucks, one of which had a long wand spraying a mist of chemicals into trees along the road: maple, oak, pine, spruce, catalpa, walnut, and others.

I'd already noticed the results of spraying in Pennsylvania: a brown swath of dead vegetation along the east-west road that runs through my town—Route 30 or the famous Lincoln Highway, America's first transcontinental highway. And I've seen masses of brown vegetation along the Pennsylvania turnpike. Now my road was being hit with herbicides.

What Would Rachel Carson Say?

"There is a steadily growing chorus of outraged protest about the disfigurement of once beautiful roadsides by chemical sprays, which substitute a sere expanse of brown, withered vegetation for the beauty of fern and wildflower, of native shrubs adorned with blossom or berry."

Rachel Carson spent her childhood on the other side of Pittsburgh about fifty miles from here. She lived, as I do now, in a white nineteenth-century farmhouse with a spring house and a grape arbor. But there our commonality ends. She was arguably the most influential environmentalist of the twentieth century. I am simply one who admires her book, *Silent Spring*, published in 1962—and not just because it led to the ban of DDT, but because Carson wrote about science in such a poetic way. Sixty-one years later we are still spraying chemicals on the roadsides in the state where Carson was born.

What Would Rachel Carson Say?

"Hedgerows along country roads and bordering fields provide food, cover, and nesting areas for birds and homes for many wild animals. . . . Such vegetation is also the habitat of wild bees and other pollinating insects. Man is more dependent on these wild pollinators than he usually realizes."

I called Pennsylvania's Department of Transportation (PennDOT) and was told by a district roadside specialist that they're allowed to spray due to a June 1945 State Highway Law. PennDOT conducts three herbicide programs, which, according to their Herbicide Use Position paper, is "to maintain a safe travel way that is free from obstructing vegetation." Their literature states that they have 150,000 acres of right-of-way to maintain and serve twelve million people with different opinions. "The Department of Transportation seeks understanding and support for this program."

One of those three state programs was in progress on my road that day. A company subcontracted by PennDOT was spraying what the roadside specialist called "a bud inhibitor," which prevents buds from forming on trees the next season. He sent me the chemical company fact sheet that states, "Only protected handlers may be in the area during application," and agricultural workers are not to enter "into treated areas during the restricted entry interval (REI) of 12 hours."

We were not informed our road was to be sprayed. How do we know, then, to stay out of the area during spraying or for twelve hours afterward? We might have been walking in a field that borders Route 711. My husband had just mown around the perimeter. For years we had cows there.

There is no way to let everyone know, the roadside specialist said. I suggested putting notices in the newspaper or a public service announcement on the radio. Impossible, he said. What about social media, telephone calls, a moveable neon sign—a megaphone? (Somehow, politicians manage to get ahold of me by telephone and mass mailings every election year.) Because I have a right to know.

What Would Rachel Carson Say?
"If the Bill of Rights contains no guarantee that a citizen shall be secure against lethal poisons distributed either by private individuals or by public officials, it is surely only because our forefathers, despite their considerable wisdom and foresight, could conceive of no such problem."

The chemical company recommends that handlers follow label directions to minimize spray drift because "this product may adversely impact the forage and habitat of local pollinators, including the monarch butterfly (and its larvae), birds, or bats if it reaches non-target areas." I find it ironic that PennDOT recently issued a new license plate to raise money for a Pollinator Habitat Program Fund to "create naturalized gardens and meadows planted with pollinator-friendly species of flowering plants specifically for bees, butterflies, beetles, and other insects which may have been adversely affected by the loss of their native habitat." And yet we spray herbicide that can harm pollinators.

I asked the roadside specialist if, instead of spraying, branches might be cut and weeds mown? Spraying saves a lot of money, he said, is safer for his crews and motorists. PennDOT's literature backs that up: "Herbicide use is more cost-effective than tree cutting or trimming." He said Pennsylvania uses the best chemicals and applies them judiciously, uses the best management practices, and puts out the best program they can to protect the driving public.

What Would Rachel Carson Say?
"It is cheaper than mowing, they cry. . . . So perhaps it appears in the neat rows of figures in the official books; but were the true costs entered . . . the wholesale broadcasting of chemicals would be seen to be more costly in dollars as well as infinitely damaging to the long-range health of the landscape and to all the varied interests that depend on it."

Might I put a "NO SPRAY" sign on my property? Not in his district, he said. The only way they won't spray is if homeowners maintain their properties properly. The literature states, "The Department may negotiate, on a case by case basis, a Vegetation Management Permit (M-688) whereby the abutting property owner would be responsible for vegetation control in return for the

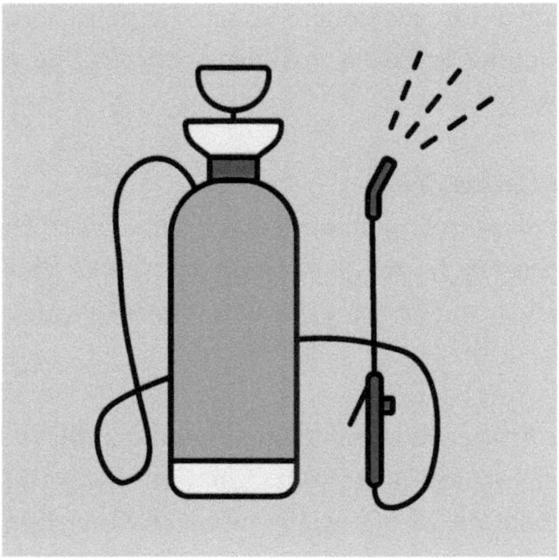

Department not using herbicide spraying. This permit would require an indemnification agreement supported by insurance in an amount sufficient to cover any Department liability."

The literature states further that I may get additional information about pesticide safety from "the PA Dept of Environmental Protection located in Harrisburg at the Rachael [*sic*] Carson State Office Building."

What Would Rachel Carson Say?
"Who has made the decision that sets in motion these chains of poisonings, this ever-widening wave of death that spreads out, like ripples when a pebble is dropped into a still pond?"

The roadside specialist told me we'd been on the phone for forty-three minutes—he was timing me—and that I was similar to only one of four people who usually call his office. I didn't know what he meant. One in four people don't yell at him, he said. I didn't want to yell, I said, I just wanted to learn. We spoke for another fifteen minutes, and while it was clear we had different opinions on this issue, I don't blame him. It's not his fault; it's the fault of the Commonwealth of Pennsylvania, which needs to figure out how to stop spraying chemicals on our roadways.

What Would Rachel Carson Say?
"The choice, after all, is ours to make. If, having endured much, we have at last asserted our 'right to know,' and if knowing, we have concluded that we are being asked to take senseless and frightening risks, then we should no longer accept the counsel of those who tell us that we must fill our world with poisonous chemicals; we should look about and see what other course is open to us."

Let us not forget that section 127 of Pennsylvania's constitution, drafted in 1967 shortly after *Silent Spring* was published and ratified in 1971, states, "The people have a right to clean air, pure water, and to the preservation of the natural, scenic, historic and esthetic values of the environment. Pennsylvania's public natural resources are the common property of all the people, including generations yet to come. As trustee of these resources, the Commonwealth shall conserve and maintain them for the benefit of all the people."

And it's not just Pennsylvania. Montana youth recently won a lawsuit that focused on that state's constitution that guarantees residents "a clean and healthful environment in Montana for present and future generations."

What Would Rachel Carson Say?
"We must remain vigilant, we must continue to challenge and to question, we must insist that the burden of proof is on those who would use these chemicals to prove the procedures are safe."

I love to walk the fields and forests of our Pennsylvania farm and I wanted to walk the sixty-five acres of fields and forests at the Rachel Carson Homestead in Springdale—where Rachel Carson's mother taught her about the natural world. But there are no fields and forests left, just a little over a half acre. Still, I was pleased to set my feet where hers had stepped, to imagine what her life there must have been like during the early part of the twentieth century. The museum's executive director told me that it was on this Pennsylvania property that Carson first developed her sense of wonder—the inspiration for her writing—and it was because of Carson's words that the world owes her such gratitude.

What would Rachel Carson say about Pennsylvania's roadside spraying today?

I think she'd turn the question on us: What kind of world are we leaving to our children?

When the Rains Come

I AM AFRAID OF THE SOUND OF RAIN.

Not a drizzle, a pitter-patter, or, as the Irish say, a fine soft day. I'm afraid of the roar of a relentless rain and a raging creek—the deluge that precedes the flood. A sound so loud I can yell at someone five feet across the creek and they can barely hear me. When I can't distinguish between what is rain and what is creek. Because I, and others who live far from a coast, have been hit by devastating floods of late—here in Pennsylvania, in Kentucky, West Virginia, and Vermont, to name a few.

I'm particularly afraid in the middle of the night when I'm home alone. Because one person cannot stop the water.

When the rains come at night, I look out our bedroom window where even in the dark I can often judge from the contour of our serpentine creek how much it is swelling and how high it has jumped its bank. But I can't tell if the pond has breached or whether the dock is submerged, signs that the house is in danger. So, I go a little crazy, race around the inside of the house checking likely access points. I flick on the outside lights to see how close the water is to the basement door. Sleep does not come easily.

The creek is close. It runs alongside the house, in front of the barn and next to the driveway, but the creek is not the only problem. Water races so fast down our steep driveway that it becomes a second river, jumps a stonewall, turns that wall into a waterfall and a flagstone patio into a swimming pool. Terra-cotta flower pots are picked up, flipped over, and swept downhill. The combination of creek and newly formed river leaves a path of destruction: fallen tree limbs, rocks, uprooted plants, and so much sediment that the pond turns the color of chocolate milk.

I was not afraid of the sound of rain until one day about twenty years ago when my children and I were watching a movie in the basement of this old farmhouse and one of them said, "Mom, what's that noise?" and the water overtook us. The downstairs bedroom was flooded, my husband's office, and the laundry room. The water just kept coming. We'd never had that happen before.

We live partway up the mountain so it's not as bad for us as for those who live along the river in the middle of town. When the rains come, I think of

my children's saintly first-grade teacher, who lives on the banks of Loyalhanna Creek. I shudder to think of what she and her family go through every time.

Floods in western Pennsylvania are not new. We have lots of rivers and the terrain is hilly. Forty-five minutes away from here is the site of Pennsylvania's most famous flood, the Johnstown Flood of 1889, a horrendous flood that took the lives of 2,209 people. But we've lived here for thirty-six years and the drenching rains come more frequently now, often with high winds, fallen trees, and a loss of power. Flash flood warnings are frequent.

The timing is changing too. Once the floods came in May or June, maybe July, but last August—usually our dry month—we had a flood, and we just avoided one in April. I was driving on Route 30, the old Lincoln Highway, where I saw newly formed waterfalls cascading down the hills into the gorge. Smaller roads were closed, buses thwarted, and school cancelled. Pittsburgh, an hour away, broke its daily rainfall record on April 9 with 2.77 inches of rain. The first twelve days of April saw more rain in Pittsburgh than any month on record.

This original part of this old house, built about 1860, is made of logs, large beams, and a stone fireplace. It was placed on a dirt road at the bottom of three hills, out of the wind, where farmers sited houses then. It was not built to withstand today's storms, but still, we've tried our best to preserve it, to keep the water at bay.

In the basement bedroom there was a clue that the previous owner—who lived here from the 1940s until the 1980s—may have had a problem with water as there was a strip of metal at the bottom of the door. But our problem is so much worse now that we had to change that door into a window. We created a swale to divert the water away from the house and, at a basement window, placed an unsightly row of sand bags that intermingle with my white tulips. We added drains along the driveway that we check assiduously before a storm to make sure they are not clogged with leaves or sticks.

The water from our unnamed and seemingly inconsequential little creek runs into the Loyalhanna, which meets the Conemaugh, forms the Kiskiminetas, joins the Allegheny, flows into the Ohio and then the Mississippi—all of which ends up in the Gulf of Mexico. We hear all the time about sea level rise, but those of us who live inland are connected by creeks and streams and rivers.

When the rains come, I bet they too have come to dread sounds they once loved—of rain on the roof, a rising creek, a crack of thunder—the sounds of an impending storm.

Poison Ivy

One of my husband's first tasks when we moved to the farm thirty-six years ago was to remove poison ivy from the trees. He never used chemicals, just his two (gloved) hands. He came home time and time again with poison ivy pustules on his wrists that leaked liquid for three weeks. "A fool's errand," he said.

A fool's errand not just because poison ivy is difficult to eradicate, but because the plant apparently doesn't usually harm trees. I thought it did; I'd read that poison ivy blocks the sun, weakens trees, and weighs down branches that break more easily in high wind. But Susan Pell, poison ivy expert and executive director of the US Botanic Garden in Washington, DC, said not necessarily. Poison ivy might harm young or sick trees, she said, but "the native species in the forest have evolved together so it's not really a big issue."

For those allergic to poison ivy—and that's 80 to 90 percent of us—it may be disconcerting to learn that poison ivy is thriving due to climate change. Many woody plants grow better with more carbon dioxide in the atmosphere—and poison ivy stands out. In a six-year study at the Duke University Forest, carbon dioxide was pumped artificially into a controlled setting to mimic climate scenarios. "Poison ivy was the fastest growing of all plants studied," Pell said. It topped the chart, growing 70 percent faster. Its leaves grew larger, and the urushiol—the oily ingredient that causes the rash—became more virulent.

All it takes to get a rash from poison ivy is the slightest touch or "50 micrograms of urushiol, an amount that is less than one grain of table salt," according to the Centers for Disease Control. Every part of the plant is poisonous, Pell said, but "the rash is not directed at us." Urushiol may protect the plant itself against infection as urushiol is anti-bacterial and anti-fungal.

Poison ivy also has a host of redeeming qualities. Its berries—or drupes—are food for many birds. Deer, black bear, rabbits, and other animals eat the plant (they disperse the seeds; the plant spreads by rhizomes too). Some insects eat the plant and poison ivy's leaves provide shelter for them. It helps prevent erosion.

The plant's Latin name, *Toxicodendron radicans*, means "poison tree" and it is in the Anacardiaceae, or cashew family, which includes mango, pistachio, sumac, and smoke tree. Many poisonous plants exist in that family, but "poison ivy is the most notorious," Pell said. The plant grows in every state except California, in disturbed areas such as pathways and the forest edge where light is more abundant. It comes in many forms: as a groundcover; as a large vine called a liana; and as a shrub. I've never seen the shrub version, but Pell has: six feet high on the New Jersey coast with slick black bark. On our farm, we have lianas—the kind my husband was tackling—so big and hairy and when they climb a tree their leaves are difficult to distinguish from those of the host tree.

Poison ivy is a Pennsylvania native and is being studied here too, but in a different manner. Mason Heberling, associate curator of botany at the Carnegie Museum of Natural History, has retrieved from the museum's herbarium, 327 specimens of poison ivy, poison sumac, staghorn sumac, and Virginia creeper, all collected across Pennsylvania from 1838 to 2020. By looking at dried and pressed leaves, flowers, and branches, he's confirmed that with increased CO_2, poison ivy has "shifted several traits." (Heberling said CO_2 measured around 285 parts per million in the nineteenth century and today is nearly 420 parts per million and "rising each year.") Leaf size has increased, the number of pores on the leaves has decreased, and its water use has declined. His results were published in the *American Journal of Botany*, and while he's not yet sure what those results mean exactly, he'll continue to study what he called an undercollected and understudied plant.

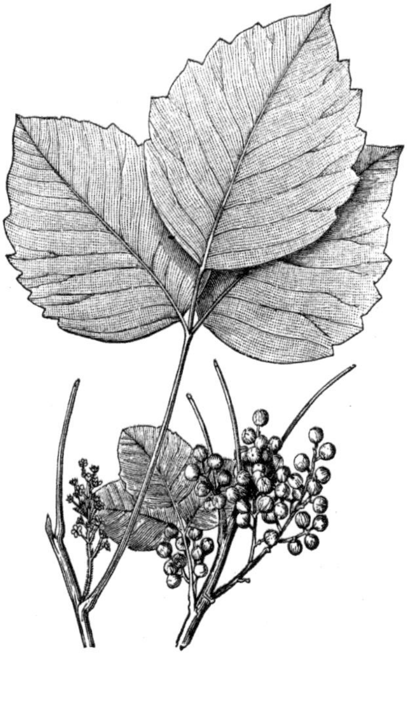

The leading explanation for poison ivy's fast growth is because of its vining habit, Heberling said. The plant doesn't have to invest as much energy into making wood and "cheats by climbing up trees," he said. Such increased vigor may indeed harm forests in the future. According to Duke, "Rising CO_2 is potentially responsible for the increased vine abundance that is inhibiting forest regeneration and increasing tree mortality around the world."

Poison Ivy is a common allergen and researchers worry that with faster growth and increased urushiol, people will get rashes more easily and have more severe attacks. The best thing, of course, is to avoid the plant, but to do so one must be able to recognize it and identification can be tricky. The common adage "Leaves of three, let it be" is meant to help us, but Pell has seen poison ivy with five leaflets—the scientific term—in Boston and Texas. Leaves can be large or small, shiny or dull, margined or lobed, and, in autumn, they turn a brilliant red, one of the first plants to change color. "One thought is that the bright red leaves of fall are to attract migrating birds to its fruit," Heberling said. Look-alikes include Virginia creeper, blackberry, and box elder.

Pell thinks it's important for everyone to recognize poison ivy. "It's common in so many areas in which people spend time that almost everyone in the eastern US is likely to encounter it," she said. "People often think of it being only in and near forests, but it's also at the beach growing in the dunes, in yards and gardens, and in urban areas. I've seen it growing over and along bike paths, growing on fences along sidewalks, and at train stations in numerous cities, and even growing out of roof gutters."

One problem may be what's called "plant blindness," when people don't recognize plants or can't tell one plant from another. "People don't see the diversity in front of them," Pell said. "Some people don't understand that plants are even alive. That's a big issue from a conservation standpoint. If people can't recognize a plant, they can't appreciate it."

People also don't realize that poison ivy can remain on clothes, garden tools, and pet fur for a long time. Plants are poisonous even in winter and dried plants can transmit the rash. Fires can cause urushiol to get into lungs, so don't burn it, and don't weed-whack it. According to Penn State, the best way to control poison ivy is "repeatedly amputating the vine at its source." That's my husband's method.

Pell recommends washing affected areas with old-fashioned soap and water, preferably cold. Hot water opens the skin's pores and allows urushiol to enter more easily. Being fond of natural remedies, I have often rubbed jewelweed—which can grow near poison ivy—on my skin after exposure, but I was disappointed to learn from Pell that jewelweed does not counter the urushiol.

Three and a half decades later, my husband no longer gets poison ivy. He spends at least as much time, if not more, in the forest, and believes he's built up an immunity, but Pell said science doesn't support his theory. On the other hand, she has heard anecdotes of lighter symptoms, or hyposensitization, occurring in people who work in the lacquer industry, where urushiol is harvested from the Japanese lacquer tree to create lacquerware.

Only time—and exposure—will tell.

An Ode on Snow Days

When I was young, one of the best two-word combinations in the English language was *snow day*!

When I didn't have to go to school and could stay in my pajamas and watch tv. When I coaxed myself into bulky pants, jackets, socks and boots—way before fleece, down, and waterproof fabric—and my feet got sopped in five minutes anyway. I found the dusty sled in the garage and hauled it outside with my siblings and the sled got stuck for the first few runs until the blades were cold and accustomed to doing what they were designed to do. I made snow angels and watched dogs leap through piles of snow higher than they were. I ate snow dribbled with maple syrup, had snowball fights, and built snowmen with carrot noses and old scarves around their necks. It felt daring to walk straight down the middle of a street too snowy for cars. Maybe my dad didn't go to work because his car couldn't make it to the train station so he played with us on a school day and mom had hot cocoa with marshmallows ready when we came inside with icy fingers and red at the tips of our noses.

When my children were young, we still had snow days. I remember a stretch of them when I was on a predawn "call list" to inform other parents that school was cancelled in Ligonier. We had enough snow on this Pennsylvania farm to snowshoe or cross-country ski and ice thick enough to skate on the pond. A friend brought a carriage, hitched it to one of our horses, and we rode across

the fields. One winter night with a full moon my husband pulled children up our big hill on the ATV and they sledded down. Our rural school had a tradition whereby everyone got out early on Friday afternoons to go skiing at our local ski resort, and sometimes the snowmaking machines were not turned on.

But do children even have snow days anymore? Is it just my imagination or are snow days waning? I asked a snow expert.

"From my own experience we haven't had as many snow days," said Elizabeth Burakowski, a research assistant professor who studies the effects of climate change on snow at the University of New Hampshire's Earth Systems Research Center. Her family has had "nor'easter days," she said, when it rains and power lines are down, or heat days when classrooms are eighty degrees and there's no air conditioning. "Not as much fun as snow days," she said.

For those of us who love snow, the statistics are depressing. In a 2019 study by Hubbard Brook Research Foundation in Woodstock, Vermont, seventeen researchers collected data from weather stations across the northeastern United States, eastern Canada, and the Great Lakes. "Winters in the eastern areas of the northern forest have lost about 21 days of snow cover over the past century," they concluded. Researchers also saw an increase in "mud days" when the ground is bare and daytime temperatures go above freezing.

"The Northeast United States is a hotspot for heating in winter," Burakowski said. Burlington, Vermont, is getting warmer fastest, followed by Albany, Georgia; Chattanooga, Tennessee; Milwaukee, Wisconsin; and Concord, New Hampshire.

Snow is important for reasons other than snow days. According to the National Snow and Ice Data Center, snow cools the planet by reflecting sunlight back into space. It is an insulator that protects tree roots and soil microbes. Snow affects hibernating animals and migratory birds, drinking water and irrigation. Lack of snow can increase forest fires and expand invasive forest pests. Local economies, such as ski resorts, depend on snow.

The list is a lot longer.

Burakowski and her colleagues looked at twenty-nine different climate models to project how much snow we might have by the end of the century. They used two scenarios: high level CO_2 emissions in the atmosphere (without the 2015 Paris Agreement) and low levels (maintaining 2021 climate policies). Between 1980 and 2005, the number of snow-covered days in the Northeast was ninety-five days. By 2100, in a low-emissions scenario, the Northeast would have seventy-two days of snow cover, but with higher emissions, only fifty-six days. In Connecticut, where I had many childhood snow days, we used to get twenty to eighty days of snow, but with the higher emissions, we'd have no snow at all.

Solastalgia is a word coined by Australian philosopher Glenn Albrecht that combines the words *solace* and *algia* and means the distress caused by environmental changes close to home. That's the way I feel about our lack of snow on the farm. But it's more than that. Snow days are one of the wonders of childhood and I'm sad our youngest generation is missing out on that same joy. My generation owes them more than just an apology; we owe them action. Fixing the problem shouldn't be theirs alone. We are flying down a big hill with obstacles in the way, but it's not too late to steer our sled in another direction.

Spring Blooming Plants Blooming in Fall

It's the holiday season and my rural Pennsylvania town is bursting with the signs of Christmas: wreaths hung on doors, trees strung with colorful lights, a creche erected in the town square—and spring-flowering plants in bloom.

My forsythia is blooming a bright yellow. White lilacs are just dying back. Pink magnolia buds have recently faded.

"This is the first year I've seen honeysuckle bloom in fall," said Mason Heberling, associate curator of botany at the Carnegie Museum of Natural History in Pittsburgh. And forsythia "is extra weird this year," he said. "Other botanists—in person and online—are talking about this too." Such untimely blooms have caused Heberling to pause and ask himself, "What season is it?"

What season indeed? I am not a botanist, just a gardener and an observer of plants on a farm in the Appalachian foothills, but in thirty-five years, I've never seen all these plants rebloom in fall.

The lilac was an odd sight, so strange that those of us on the farm mentioned it to each other: *Did you see the lilac in bloom?* Little white tufts resembling cotton balls sat atop nearly leafless branches. Most of the leaves had turned color and fallen to the ground, but the flowers were blooming.

It was a partial, not a full bloom, what Heberling called "a muted response," but still, it was unnerving to see plants that normally flower in spring bloom again at Thanksgiving—and now, nearly Christmas. It felt a bit out of a science fiction thriller, but I think I was just witnessing climate change in my own backyard. And I think many people won't believe climate change until they *too* see it in their own backyards.

"False spring," Heberling called it. "These plants are confused for a variety of reasons."

Nonnative plants are the rebloomers, Heberling said. Most plants respond to three main phenological cues that trigger bud burst in spring: duration of winter cold (chilling requirements), changing day length, and warming temperatures. When any one of these three is out of whack, strange things can happen. And since nonnatives require less chilling than native plants, they may get tricked more easily.

Take the nonnative lilac. The shrub produces new buds in early summer after spring flowers have faded and holds onto those buds over winter. But when the plant is faced with environmental stresses such as drought or heat, it can go into dormancy early. Then, when there's a warm snap, plants are fooled into thinking it is spring and begin to bloom.

Last summer's weather offered its fair share of drought and heat, now "the new normal." We had nearly three weeks with no rain at all and then a flood in August, which is usually our dry month. Planet Earth saw the hottest meteorological summer on record in 2023 (until it was followed by 2024).

But warmer winter temperatures are what are reflected in the new USDA Plant Hardiness Zone Map, just released. To determine gardening zones, the United States Department of Agriculture measured the coldest temperature on the coldest night of the year over a thirty-year period. The 2023 map reflects 2.5 degrees F (1.4 degrees C) warmer temperatures since the map was last published in 2012. About half our country shifted warmer a half zone, including my zone in the Laurel Highlands, which went from a 5b to a 6a.

"This is a big deal," Heberling said. "Climate is changing to the point that we can plant garden plants that can only grow in milder winters that we couldn't plant before. And more significant, that means that native plants can also shift. Things are up in the air as we enter new climate space."

The general consensus is that my reblooming shrubs will not be harmed. Those fall blooms, however, will not rebloom in spring, which might make next year's display less spectacular. The scientists I spoke to said there's still a lot they don't understand about how changing climatic conditions will affect plant blooms, but Heberling said, "I do suspect we will have more oddities in the timing of flowering as weather and climate become more irregular."

"Enjoy the fall flowers," he said.

What I Learned from My Compost Heap

Of all the jobs I do in my garden—hoeing, sowing, weeding, mulching—the one I've always avoided was turning the compost heap. Our compost heap is huge and the task is difficult, so whenever our friend with a backhoe came to help us with a farm chore, I always whispered: *Might you sneak over and turn the compost?* But then my husband redesigned the compost heap so the tractor bucket could fit inside and do the heavy lifting for us. He surrounded the pile with a concrete retaining wall, which he faced with stone. When we look at the compost heap from the kitchen window now, it resembles a lovely New England stone wall.

But last summer, the tractor broke, and in autumn, it still sat in a million pieces in the shop. I needed compost for the usual fall transplanting, but more so this year because my plants had been stripped of topsoil. In August, we had yet another of what we once called "the 100-year flood." We've had about

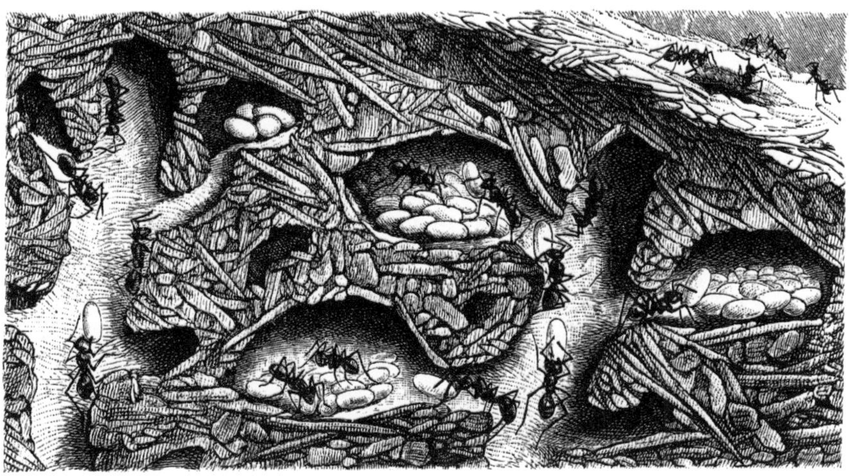

eight of those in the last twenty years where water cascades down our driveway and turns a stone wall into a waterfall and creates a mote around this old Pennsylvania farmhouse. Previous floods had come in May, June, and July, but this one surprised us in August, usually our dry month. Making matters worse, we'd just added mulch to the gardens, which was carried down the stream and into the pond.

Our compost heap includes leaves, grass clippings, kitchen scraps, chicken and horse manure, dog hair, cardboard, and newspaper. Every time I dump in an armful of shredded cardboard or a bucket of coffee grounds, I think how fortunate I am to be able to put back into the earth the waste that others toss into garbage cans. I love that I don't add as much to the landfill—and that my detritus turns into "black gold" strikes me as some sort of marvel. But during the tractor's absence, weeds had taken over, and in autumn, we'd tossed on top mounds of pumpkin, nasturtium, and morning glory vines from the vegetable garden, making the pile harder to turn by hand.

There must be a compost god because then an old friend came to visit. His car broke down and, worrying he was overstaying his welcome, offered to help around the farm. I loaned him some muck boots and on a fine fall day we climbed atop what had become a compost mountain. He had a fork, I, a shovel, and as we dug, lifted, turned, and groaned, we talked of memories of a college semester in Paris. There's something about manual labor that cements a friendship.

When he left, I was on my own—along with three dogs–mucking around in dirt. One thing I could do that a tractor couldn't was remove errant rubber bands, terra-cotta pot shards, fruit tags, and plastic plant markers. Temperatures cooled and the leaves turned red and yellow. A pileated woodpecker swooped overhead. One evening I stood still to listen to a great horned owl call from the hilltop.

I grabbed a handful of moist soil, crumbled it in my hand and smelled it—purposely breathing in geosmin, an earthy scent believed to be calming, as psychiatrist Sue Stuart-Smith writes in *The Well-Gardened Mind*. There was no tractor noise, no use of fossil fuel. I was happy out there, helping to create soil. But I was just a bit player on a bigger stage.

The real work was being done by the decomposers below my feet: the beetles, millipedes, snails, slugs, ants, and the earthworms, which Aristotle called the "intestines of the earth." Those that chew, shred, decompose, excrete, tunnel, aerate—all while nourishing our soil.

My favorites are the pill bugs, not insects at all but crustaceans that live their entire lives on land, breathe through gills, and have seven pairs of legs. And there was more than that—an entire ecosystem I couldn't see with the naked eye, microorganisms such as bacteria, nematodes, fungi, springtails, and mites, working their magic.

"Without those organisms, leaves would just be dead leaves and would never turn into soil," said John Wenzel, an entomologist at the Conemaugh Valley Conservancy. "We wouldn't have a terrestrial environment we recognize without them."

This fall, a broken tractor forced me to slow down, pay attention, and meditate on soil brimming with life. What these tiniest of creatures do for us seems nothing short of a miracle and I, for one, am grateful.

We ask so much of them, yet how do we treat them in return? We dump pesticides on them. Insecticides. Herbicides. And fertilizers. I rototill.

What would they say, I wonder, if they could speak? What might they ask of us in return?

HOME AND GARDEN

Dreams of the Possible and Impossible for This Year's Garden

The silent season has begun. The garden is put to bed, herbs cut back and hung in the barn, the last of the sorrel eaten and the first of the Jerusalem artichokes. Flowers are mulched with shredded leaves, boxwood wrapped in burlap, snow fence draped around shrubs to prevent deer from devouring them. Few birds are left: juncos, cardinals, blue jays, red-bellied woodpeckers at the feeder—but little of their music to lift my heart. There is an occasional caw of a crow, the chickadee-dee-dee of a chickadee, the big song of the little Carolina wren that now stays on our Pennsylvania farm all winter—but no courtship call of great horned owls, no wood thrush or Baltimore oriole. Still, I rejoice in what remains.

Deer have turned the color of milk chocolate to dark chocolate. Squirrels still race around adding to their larders, but the chipmunks are mostly gone, in their dens I suppose, along with the opossum, raccoons, and the bears too.

Once I longed for a greenhouse, but now I too want to hibernate—to take time off from potting, sowing, and nurturing. To walk in snowy woods and observe animal tracks, study ice patterns on the pond, to be one with the season. I want to read by the fire and imagine what next year's garden will be

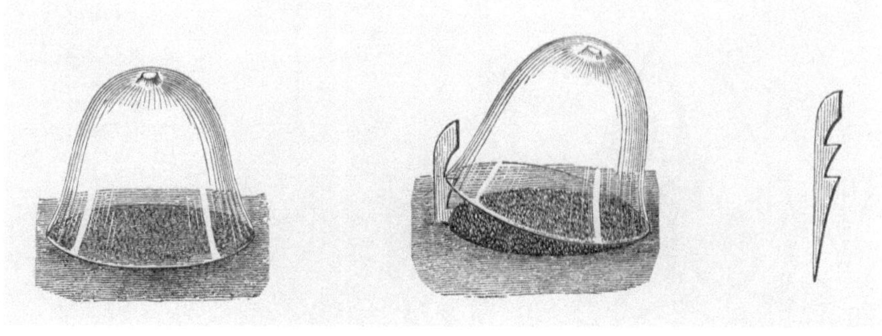

like—expecting, as all gardeners do, that next year will be better than the last. To go through garden catalogues and dream, such as writer and gardener Vita Sackville-West wrote in her poem:

Winter:
. . . The gardener dreams his special own alloy
Of possible and the impossible . . .

But what is possible anymore? As I reflect on last year's abysmal gardening season, I wonder how I will adapt to the changes I witness.

Last winter was so warm that shrubs hardly died back and, in spring, dripped with foliage—a welcome sight, but not normal. Spring was so hot I missed that lovely, cool, window for transplanting. I didn't know when to plant early-season, cold-hardy vegetables—certainly not in eighty-five degrees—or when to set out tender plants. "After danger of frost" is common wisdom, but when is that now? My USDA Plant Hardiness Zone changed recently from 5b to 6a, but I'm still confused. Mid-May felt like mid-June—and then we had hail on May 29.

I planted poppies in April anyway—they like cool weather—but the seeds were washed away by floods, which can now stretch here from April through

October. Between June and November, we had a severe drought. The grass was brown. Dogwood and tulip poplar lost their leaves in July. My vegetable garden resembled a cracked riverbed, the soil so hard that weeding was nearly impossible.

Streams ran dry so for the first time in thirty-six years I saw deer wade into the pond to drink. Little food was available for them either so they sauntered up to our garage and ate the "deer resistant" lavender. On my walks in the forest, I was struck by a lack of undergrowth, particularly a huge patch of Canadian wood nettle, a North America native that is a host plant for red admiral and eastern comma butterflies. Chanterelles never fruited in their usual spots. I worried our spring would run dry.

Pennsylvania saw record wildfires in fall, when two lilacs bloomed, and in late November I was still harvesting what little I did manage to grow. The year 2024 was the warmest on record, when temperatures rose above 1.5 Celsius.

All this reminds me of a radio program called *Piano Puzzler* that my husband and I listen to on Saturday mornings. Composer Bruce Adolphe rewrites a familiar tune in the style of a classical composer—think "Danny Boy" in the style of Bach. He changes the tune's tempo, harmony, or mode and contestants try to name the tune and composer. Somewhere in my brain the tune sounds familiar, yet something is off, the music is disorienting. Occasionally, I guess correctly, often not. Gardening in climate change is the same: confusing, with a lot of guessing.

What's a home gardener to do? I ask an expert.

"The only predictable thing is that it is going to be unpredictable," said Sonja Skelly, director of education at Cornell Botanic Gardens. "It's been crazy up here too."

Drip irrigation is one solution, Skelly said. "It adds moisture where it's needed, at the roots," she said. Water is released slowly, stays put, and doesn't run off like hand watering or using sprinklers.

Last spring was hot in Ithaca too so the vegetable gardener planted vegetables two weeks before their May 31 frost-free date. Then came extreme temperature fluctuations, but the plants set out earlier did better because they got established. Those planted on the proper date were stunted and had a poor growing season. "A good lesson," Skelly said. Row covers, which allow gardeners to get plants in earlier and grow them later in the season, are "going to be really important in climates like ours," she said.

Cover crops such as millet, sorghum, and black-eyed peas have been successful there. They slow water retention, decrease weeds, reduce erosion, and limit negative microorganisms in soil. The birds loved them, Skelly said.

She recommended planting together the Haudenosaunee trio called "the three sisters": corn, beans, and pumpkin. This system produces a better per hectare yield than any monoculture cropping system, she said. And to kill pests and weeds without chemicals, Skelly suggested soil solarization, a method that uses landscape fabric and the sun's heat to eradicate them.

"Observe, take notes, ask questions, seek out answers," Skelly advised. "What are the neighbors seeing?" Learn by going to local botanic gardens, public gardens, and nature centers, which have been working on this problem for a while now. "Keep the cycle of information flowing, talking with friends and family and neighbors as a way to help us figure it out. That's so important," she said.

Skelly believes it's crucial for home gardeners to really understand their plants. "Maybe climate change will be the way to know our gardens far better," she said. "We have to."

I've long depended on experts to teach me how to garden responsibly—to help, not harm the environment. I don't spray pesticides or insecticides and instead of synthetic fertilizers, use compost, or I make natural fertilizers from comfrey and stinging nettle. I plant a diverse range of plants—including natives for pollinators—and I've learned to celebrate native weeds. I wish I could buy plants in something other than plastic.

But the more I ponder gardening in climate change, the more I believe we home gardeners are going to have to figure out many solutions for ourselves. So much of gardening is trial and error and erratic weather patterns mean we'll have to experiment even more, to do our own studies. In essence, we must become citizen scientists of our own vegetable patches and flower beds.

Cornell Botanic Gardens has a climate change demonstration garden, but, really, we all do. None of us has been through this before. And in the end, we're all in this together, navigating a strange new world of digging in soil and growing things, each trying as we might to contribute to a new way of gardening in a changing world.

What My Dog Taught Me About Aging

Our dog takes one step at a time every morning coming down the stairs of this old farmhouse. He has cataracts and cannot see well. Our other two dogs barrel in front of him, but Basil takes each step slowly, checks his landings carefully with his front paws. My husband or I stay close in case he slips. If he does, I'm not sure I can catch him—he is a large goldendoodle, eighty-five pounds at his heaviest—but I would throw my body in front of his if need be. Sometimes he stops and looks up at me. I pat his head. "Three more," I say. "Two more. One more, Bazzy. Good boy."

When our daughter was young, she named him after Basil Fawlty, John Cleese's character in *Fawlty Towers*. We laughed at those old television shows and our daughter could recite many passages. Our middle dog is named Sybil, for Basil Fawlty's wife. She is four years younger, small and black and she and Basil curl up together like half-moons. Every morning she too watches Basil come down the stairs. When he has three steps to go, Sybil walks back up the stairs and nudges Basil's snout. Well done, she seems to say. I am here too.

I am growing old with Basil. He is about to turn fifteen, the oldest dog we've ever had. I'm the eldest in the family and have had cataract surgery. Dr. Deepinder Dhaliwal, a superb ophthalmologist, helped me see better. My husband jokes that Basil needs Dr. Doggiwal. Dr. Dhaliwal laughed when I told her that, said she would gladly perform the surgery if she could. She had just gotten her first puppy and was learning how easily we lose our hearts to dogs.

Basil's hind end is going. His back legs don't always follow the front; they go sideways. My balance is not as good as it used to be either. Some days my hip hurts, or a foot, or a knee, and I come down the stairs one step at a time, holding tight to the railing. Basil used to run up our long driveway at 22 mph following my husband on the all-terrain vehicle. When we played keep-away, Basil turned like a cutting horse, so quick we couldn't catch him. My usual walk in the woods with all three dogs includes three hills, but now, without words, Basil makes clear he is willing to climb two hills maximum. He takes short cuts. Some days one hill is enough and he opts for a ride home with my husband in the back of our pickup truck. At the steepest parts of the hills, Basil huffs and puffs. So do I.

We have had many dogs since we moved to the farm: Bernese mountain dogs, giant schnauzers, golden retrievers, and now two goldendoodles and a schnoodle. Of all the dogs, Basil is the most Zen. If another dog wants a bone or a toy, he gives it to them. If another dog wants to go through a door first, he waits patiently. Basil allows the other dogs to eat before he does. Children can sit on top of him. He reminds me to be more selfless and kindhearted.

Four years ago this Memorial Day, we thought we'd lost him. He couldn't walk. We guessed he'd had a stroke. He wouldn't eat or drink, seemed disoriented. Sometimes I too am disoriented. I walk into a room and am not sure what I'm seeking there. I have odd ailments that appear suddenly. My husband carried Basil down the stairs and outside, lay on the ground, and stroked him. We told Basil everything would be OK. I have seldom seen my husband cry. We called the children, let them say goodbye over the phone.

A friend saved his life. She said when her dog had a stroke a vet told her that while the stroke might not kill him, dehydration could, so to give him electrolytes. I raced to a convenience store and fed him electrolytes through a turkey baster. Since then he has been on high blood pressure medicine. I do not take high blood pressure medicine, but I take my fair share of remedies.

We got a puppy and Basil was young again. Sometimes old dogs respond enthusiastically to new puppies, our vet said. Basil tried to play keep-away again, chased the puppy at the start of our walks as the giant schnauzer had once done to him, directed the puppy to the spot in the stream where every one of our long line of dogs has drunk from a French drain. He taught the puppy what he knew.

Each morning, when Basil descends the stairs, he has, on his face, the closest a dog can have to a smile. It is a new day and he is happy to take the stairs one at a time. He is with the other dogs. He is with us. He is at the place he has always called home. Every morning he wags his long, golden tail. If that's not a lesson for aging, I don't know what is.

The World You Discover When You Garden at Night

When it's too hot to garden during the day, what is there to do but garden at night? Neither floppy hat nor gobs of sunscreen will lure me into the brilliance of a sometimes record-breaking, hot and humid, ninety-plus-degree day. Or as our local meteorologist likes to report: one with a "heat index" of 103. So instead, I venture out into the garden after dinner, dogs in tow, surveying the raised beds in the coolness of evening.

I carry a basket full of seeds, green string to tie the tomatoes higher, and wooden stakes and black markers to record once again what I have sown—some new crops and others a repeat of those planted earlier in the season. It is midsummer now and the lettuces, radishes, and shallots are fading, but the basil and tomatoes, beans and zucchini are finally coming into their own. A little more rain and warmth and I will be able to make my first tomato sandwich—tomato sandwiches no doubt being one of the driving forces behind planting a vegetable garden.

At dusk, a hush settles over the garden and reminds me of a time when I did not speak during a meditation dinner at a retreat some years ago. Eating without speaking made me notice details I wouldn't have had I been babbling: who wore a wedding ring, what morsels people left scattered on their plates. Even the food tasted different. My garden in the evening is somewhat the same.

Without the brilliance and the chatter of the day, the competing noises, the busyness and the hurry, my little plot is a deeper level of quiet, maybe even more peaceful. As much as I adore the daily refrain of eastern towhees, Carolina wrens, and baby red-tailed hawks on their first flights screaming: *Ma, Ma, look at me!* as they learn to fly, many of the feathered creatures on this farm are calling it a day too. The bees have gone quiet as well, having finished their daily sipping of borage, an herb I allow to self-sow just for them.

I do hear the whistling of the wind off the ridge, and despite the pleasures of being in the garden at night, I still pray that wind will bring rain and usher in a cold front. Maybe nighttime gardening will become one of the necessities of a warming planet.

When I garden at night, I notice entirely different aspects of the natural world. Swooping overhead I see our one lone bat, though my husband claims this summer he's seen two in the early mornings. One or two it matters not, as I know well that most of our Pennsylvania bats are gone.

I concentrate more fully on the magical twinkle of fireflies, trying to discern the males' distinctive flight pattern, looping upward like the letter J, as they look eagerly for mates during their lifespan of just three or four weeks. Watching them is extra special to me since I learned that a male might get eaten if he swoops down to a ground-dwelling female of one particular species. "Femmes fatales" the firefly experts call these predators.

A deer snorts in the woods next to garden fence; perhaps in the dark I am too close for comfort. I hear the crickets sing. "They make the hills echo," as Gilbert White wrote in *The Natural History of Selborne*. I see the first stars.

As the light fades, I plant a second crop of cilantro and arugula, guided by the bright white of four tuteurs in the garden's center. I can still see just well

enough to hoe my rows, plant my seeds, and scribble on my wooden markers. I crack open the dried pods of Shirley poppies and scatter the miniscule black seeds, imagining the coming glory of red, white, and pink poppies that will grace my garden next spring.

I call my companionable canines, willing as they are to accompany me anywhere, at any time. They do not ask why I am pulling weeds, digging garlic, or winding cucumber vines up a trellis at night. One of the three just wants me to feed her raspberries. It is so dark as I leave the garden to bid goodnight to the chickens and close the coop where they are already tucked in and I needn't round up the laggards.

As I approach the house, I see in the southeast, just above the treetops, a nearly full, brilliant orange moon begin to rise. I hear bullfrogs moan in the pond and coyotes howl in the woods. I'd like to be able to say I saw something miraculous gardening at night, a mama porcupine and her porcupette, for instance, which I'm dying to see, or at least heard the lament of the barred owl, but it is just a lovely night in a Pennsylvania vegetable garden. Isn't that miracle enough?

Reading Poems at Thanksgiving

My husband loves all the trimmings of Thanksgiving, particularly mashed potatoes. I adore my grandmother's recipe for Mamie Eisenhower's Pumpkin Chiffon Pie. But I could skip the traditional meal entirely and be perfectly happy eating takeout, because, for me, the holiday is not about food. It's about gathering together at our farm, listening to thanksgiving hymns from *Steeple on the Common*, and my favorite part of all—the poems that we read aloud around the table.

This is not an old tradition for us. I grew up in suburban New York with parents who loved the New York Giants. Thanksgiving was a typical American meal with game after game of football—sometimes between bites. There were hoots and hollers from the den, winning and losing teams, family members on opposite sides. No one thought about poetry.

But as an adult with a family of my own I began to imagine other ways to celebrate the holiday. And what better way than to pause for a few minutes to listen to the words of our poets, who remind us to be grateful for so much: for one another; the comfort of our lives compared to many; for love and justice; for children, music, and gardens; for the nature and animals that surround us; and for no wars . . . here, at least, at the moment.

Robert Louis Stevenson has welcomed us to the table:

Lord behold our family here assembled
We thank Thee for this place in which we dwell;
For the love that unites us;
For the peace accorded us this day . . .

Maya Angelou has dined with us too: "My wish for you / is that you continue / To remind the people that / Each is as good as the other / And that no one is beneath / Nor above you . . ."

We've read Czesław Milosz's "Gift": "A day so happy / Fog lifted early, I worked in the garden. / Hummingbirds were stopping over honeysuckle flowers. / There was no thing on earth I wanted to possess . . ."

And Naomi Shihab Nye, who wrote about kindness: "Before you learn the tender gravity of kindness / you must travel where the Indian in a white poncho / lies dead by the side of the road. / You must see how this could be you, / how he too was someone / who journeyed through the night with plans / and the simple breath that kept him alive . . ."

Poems are read after dinner and during dessert. Sometimes just the family is present; other times we've had larger gatherings with friends. No one has ever said no when I've requested he or she bring a poem. Everyone comes to the table with beautiful words and strong voices. Some have written their own poems, others have read classics, and there are poems we've never heard before. Some have read passages from a beloved essay; our son read an excerpt from "Walking" by Henry David Thoreau and our daughter-in-law from philosopher Emanuele Coccia: "The world is not a place; it is a state of immersion of each thing in all other things."

Elizabeth Bishop, Shakespeare, W. S. Merwin, and Mary Oliver have graced our table, as well as William Martin, who wrote of children, "Do not ask your children / to strive for extraordinary lives. / Such striving may be admirable / But it is the way of foolishness. / Help them instead to find the wonder / and the marvel of an ordinary life . . ."

During COVID, I read Pablo Neruda's "Keeping Still": "Now we count to twelve / and let's keep quiet. / For once on earth / let's not talk in any language; let's stop for one second, / and not move our arms so much. / A moment like that would smell sweet, / no hurry, no engines, / all of us at the same time / in need of rest . . ."

There was Joy Harjo's "For Calling the Spirit Back from Wandering the Earth in Its Human Feet": "Be respectful of the small insects, birds and animal people who accompany you. / Ask their forgiveness for the harm we humans have brought down upon them . . ."

And Ralph Waldo Emerson: "Write it on your heart / that every day is the best day in the year. / He is rich who owns the day, and no one owns the day / who allows it to be invaded with fret and /anxiety."

Who wouldn't welcome Wendell Berry to their feast? In his poem "The Peace of Wild Things," when he wakes in the night feeling despair, he recalls the healing power of nature:

In fear of what my life and my children's lives may be,
I go and lie down where the wood drake
Rests in his beauty on the water, and the great heron feeds.
I come into the peace of wild things . . .

Last year, our daughter went to her boyfriend's aunt's house outside Boston for the holiday. Before they arrived, the aunt emailed me and asked such a thoughtful and welcoming question: What are your Thanksgiving traditions? She wanted to surprise our daughter, to make her feel at home.

"We read poems," I said.

And so they did.

Bird Flu?

It was near dusk on an evening last spring when I looked out at the chickens from the dining room window. I was checking to see if the flock was heading toward the coop for the night. It's easier to round them up if they want to retire; if not, they run this way and that, especially a recalcitrant white Leghorn that darts away from me and forces me to chase her in circles through the mud.

They were not ready to roost.

All seemed well though: chickens doing what chickens do—scratching and pecking for bugs, rolling in the dirt, dozing on the grass in the fenced-in area of the old springhouse, now a chicken coop.

I went to the barn instead. I had chores to do there as well. I needed to water my seedlings in the garden room and feed the stray cat that took up residence in the hayloft last winter. As I walked back to the coop, I saw from a distance that one chicken was still out. Closer still, I noticed it was one of our three buff cochins—hen or rooster I wasn't sure—and it wasn't moving.

Our golden and furry-footed buff cochin rooster had dropped dead.

I can usually tell when chickens are unwell: they lose weight or drop feathers, look listless, totter across the grass, or don't leave the coop at all. I've heard them wheeze. But I'd seen no signs of distress in the rooster.

He was my prized rooster too—not because he'd won a blue ribbon at a farm show—but because I'd hatched him myself. During COVID when everyone wanted to be a chicken farmer and I couldn't order chicks from the usual Iowa hatchery, I separated the cochin rooster and hens from the flock and let nature take its course.

But raising chickens is not easy; I lost numerous chicks. The most painful loss was a chick born with one leg that stuck out lifeless behind it, called a spraddle leg. (My first mistake was naming the bird Spraddle.) It couldn't walk, could only drag itself on its belly. We tried to straighten its left leg by devising a tiny sling out of vet wrap. We built a chick hospital out of a detergent top and attached small containers of food and water so it could sit upright and feed and drink. (Mistakes two and three.)

My daughter had been home earlier in the pandemic, and she and I had witnessed a sick chick in a previous clutch. After much discussion, we had decided not to intervene, figuring the mother hen knew best how to help it. We left the peep overnight. But when we returned to the barn the next morning, it was dead. I didn't want that to happen again.

"We can judge the heart of a man by his treatment of animals," Immanuel Kant said, but now I think I shouldn't have intervened with Spraddle either. I should have let the other chickens handle a sick chick in their own manner. When Spraddle's leg didn't heal, I had the tortuous task of having to cull him from the flock. I tried to do so humanely, but that didn't work either. As I was deciding my next step, one of our dogs snatched him away and ended the affair. I dug a small grave in the woods and used a rock as a headstone. Death on the farm is never easy.

From those COVID broods, this rooster and two hens were all that remained. The rooster was stately and beautiful and since 2020 had nobly guarded a flock of eleven hens. He greeted us each morning—and throughout the day—with hardy crows. He was part of the fabric of this farm.

I turned him over to see where the attack had occurred. I looked for signs of blood, particularly the neck. I had never had a bird die so unexpectedly unless attacked by another animal, yet I doubted that had happened in the short time I was in the barn—and without the usual warning cries to which the dogs and I have become accustomed. Maybe the attack had come quickly from above: a hawk or an owl? But I saw no wound or mass of feathers. An owl usually takes the head and neck. A fox or raccoon would have eaten or taken the carcass.

Could our rooster have died of bird flu?

If so, I should not have been handling him without gloves. I went back to the barn and got a pair, returned to the coop, and did the same inspection. Still no sign of attack, which made me worry even more.

Many different strains of avian influenza have been around for a long while, but H5N1, or high pathogenic avian influenza, is widespread in wild birds and has infected poultry and dairy cows, as well as cats, dogs, foxes, bears, and other mammals. The disease was first recognized in humans in Hong Kong in 1997. As of April 2025, 972 confirmed human cases in twenty-five countries have been reported, including 470 deaths.

In the United States, seventy human cases of H5N1 have been confirmed, including one death in January 2025 of an immunocompromised man in

Louisiana. The Centers for Disease Control believes the disease is a low risk to public health.

No human deaths have been reported in Pennsylvania and we've had no cases in dairy cattle. But the Pennsylvania Department of Agriculture announced in January 2025 the first confirmed case in domestic poultry in a 50,000-bird flock on a commercial poultry farm in Lehigh County. All the birds had to be culled. Westmoreland County has had no cases, but a backyard flock in Butler County tested positive in February 2025 and six hundred birds were destroyed.

"If you suspect your birds may have avian influenza, don't wait, report it," said Heather Palm, a veterinary medical field officer with the Pennsylvania Department of Agriculture in Mercer County. She called me back after I'd called the agency's bird flu phone number in Harrisburg—open seven days a week, twenty-four hours a day. That's serious business, I thought; the government is not taking this disease lightly.

Palm confirmed what I'd read in my research—that a bird could show no symptoms and die of bird flu. "It could look like anything," she said. "Respiratory symptoms or, in hens, less egg production—or no clinical symptoms at all."

Most H5N1 infections come from waterfowl, Palm said. The disease occurs naturally in wild birds, especially ducks and geese, and spreads in their feces. But waterfowl are asymptomatic, meaning "they can carry the disease and not get sick," she said.

We have a pond and waterfowl. Last spring, we had more ducks than I could remember—our usual pair of nesting mallards and five ducklings. I loved to watch them swim across the pond like a little flotilla. Then a pair of wood ducks showed up. Canada geese land in the pond occasionally. "Just the fact that they are there is a risk," Palm said.

She asked me if I have "dedicated footwear" for the chicken coop? Yes, I said, I have a pair of old, ripped muck boots I wear in the pen—not in our house. But, she asked further, do I wear those to walk around the pond and then walk to the coop?

I do. If so, I might have picked up the disease on my boots and taken it into the henhouse. I could be the guilty one.

I also called a local chicken breeder who advised me to check the rooster's cloaca, or the vent. If that is clogged—"a pasty vent" it's called—that could be a sign of something other than bird flu—intestinal parasites, for instance, such as coccidia, a common cause of death in chickens. I did so. The vent was fine.

Palm reminded me of the necessity for safe handling—to wash my hands to prevent contracting salmonella or e coli. A neighbor had contracted salmonella from handling chicks so I am always extra careful about this, but I worried that if our rooster did have bird flu, might I have been at further risk from handling the rooster without gloves?

I'd also seen a neighbor's cat at the pond and the coop, and while Palm and I ruled out that the cat had attacked the rooster—again, there would have been signs of a struggle—that was another way the disease could have been transmitted. "Bird flu is very fatal in cats," Palm said. Cats often present with acute neurological and respiratory signs, she said.

She told me to hold on to the carcass for two days. The disease has high mortality and if the rooster had bird flu, the hens will die in the next day or two. One dead rooster wasn't a huge concern to her, but had I reported thirty thousand dead hens, Palm's team would have been out to our farm that night. And when her team visits a farm suspected of bird flu, they wear full personal protective equipment: Tyvek suits, booties, double rubber gloves, N95 respirators, and hairnets.

I waited two days. I watched the flock for further signs of death. When they were asleep in their dust holes, I worried more were dead. But in the end, all eleven hens survived. Our rooster did not have bird flu. The most likely cause of death was a heart attack, common in large breeds and five years is getting old for a big bird, Palm said. He might have had a tumor. I could have sent the carcass for a necropsy for $70, which would have given me 100 percent accuracy as to the cause of death, but Palm didn't recommend it as it wouldn't affect the rest of the flock. After two days, she said to dispose of the carcass according to what is allowed in my area.

I was grateful the rooster didn't die of bird flu, but sad to see him go. He was special to me not only because I watched his initial pips through the eggshell, but because he was gentle—to us and the hens—and the hens that will not be as safe without him. He was nearly twice their size. I've already seen the hens assume some of his duties, though, like warning of a hawk flying overhead and leading the flock in at dusk. I will watch to see which is the dominant hen in the new pecking order.

Because of bird flu, chickens are difficult to buy. The Iowa breeder had male buff cochins only and few females of any breed. A minimum order of fifteen was required to keep the chicks warm during transport and, as much as we love buff cochins, ordering fifteen roosters was not an option. I thought maybe I could replace the rooster locally, but the breeder said she couldn't find buff cochins anywhere.

The farm is quieter now—alas, no more morning avian reveille! And one less bird to round up for the night.

In Praise of a Garden

PRAISE TO THE GARDEN FOR ALL IT HAS GIVEN ME, MANY YEARS OF SOIL between my fingers and sun on my face.

For it has taught me to appreciate beauty when beauty presents itself, no matter how fleeting. When the peonies get flattened by a flash flood, I look for beauty elsewhere. I do not always wish for more.

To accept failure. I struggle to grow sweet peas, lupine, and eggplant so turn instead to plants that come more easily: runner beans, sorrel, and Jerusalem artichoke.

To appreciate the unexpected: the volunteers that survived winter—the poppy or cleome, nigella, nicotiana or borage, doing their own thing—the radicals, the free thinkers of the garden. How I love their whimsy.

Gardening has taught me to listen to the plants. They tell me when they are not living where they wish. Move them elsewhere. My aesthetic is not always their pleasure. Be patient and do not hurry them. They grow on their own schedules, not mine. And be tender with my hands—stroke them and talk to them. It matters.

Praise to the garden for the peace. When I was just out of college and working in New York City, I retreated to my parents' house in Connecticut where my mother and I gardened together. "Dirt therapy," we called it. Focusing on one task at a time—hoeing, planting, pruning, weeding, raking—is a form of meditation.

To fall in love with native weeds. Last spring, I discovered the daisy-like fleabane, a member of the aster family that attracts numerous butterflies and moths. I let it run wild.

Praise to the garden for welcoming children. I cherish the memory of my young son eating arugula by the handful and my daughter's glee at digging potatoes as if it were an Easter egg hunt.

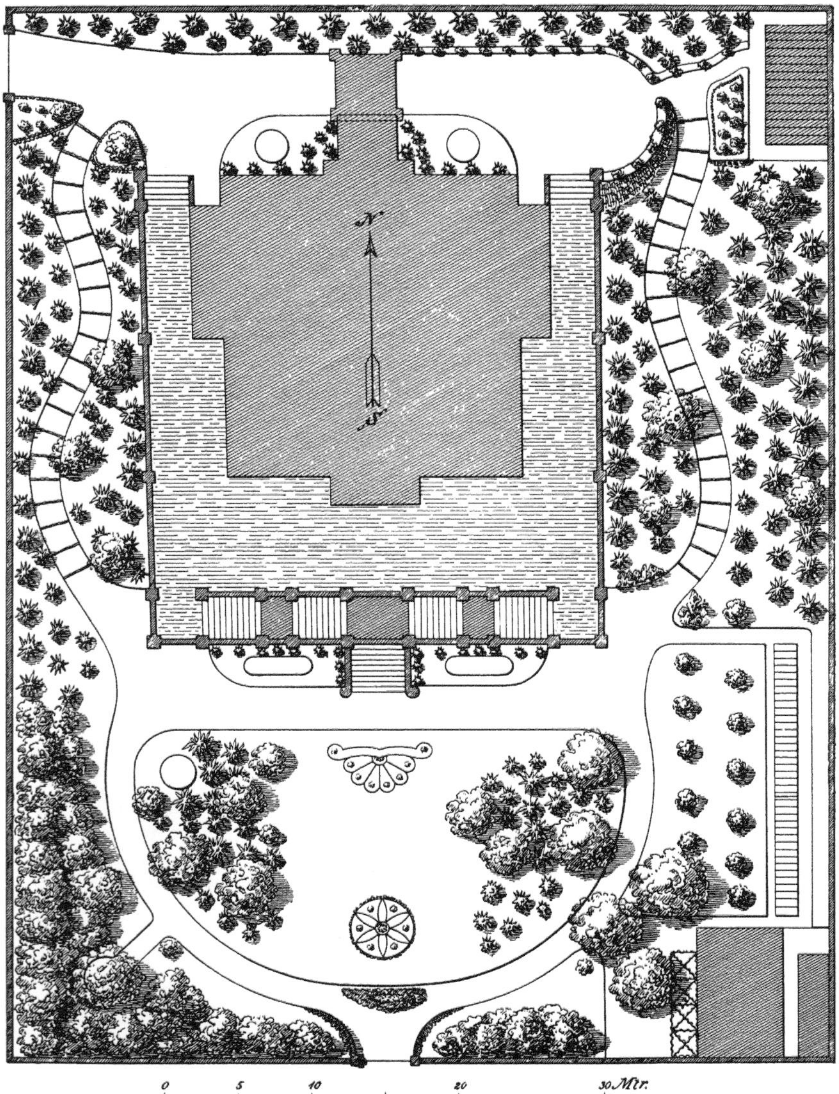
N
S
0 5 10 20 30 Mtr.

To share the fruits of my labors with the dogs, who accompany me to the vegetable garden any time of day in any weather and who sit patiently awaiting raspberries and green beans.

As a connection to my female forebears: the women who came before me, their nails also black and crusty with mud, their backs strained. A love of gardens fostered a good relationship with my mother-in-law and many friends—and here's to a gardening future with my daughter and daughter-in-law.

To employ companion planting because some plants—like people—work better together. Nasturtiums help repel squash bugs. Lettuces make radishes more tender. Sage protects against the white cabbage butterfly. Other plants are not so fond of each other. Do not plant beans and peas near shallots. Sunflowers and potatoes stunt each other's growth.

The garden taught me to eat according to the season. In summer I want zucchini, tomatoes, and peppers and do not crave broccoli and cauliflower until the weather cools.

In a garden, less really is more. If I plant too many plants too close together, I get a smaller crop.

A garden helps me help others by growing food for them, giving away plants and vegetables.

Gardening has taught me to savor anticipation. I love the vegetable garden early in the season when the beds are ready for planting, but before I've dropped a seed. I imagine broccoli without cabbage butterflies, zucchini without squash bugs, no slugs, or asparagus beetles, or tomato blight. Surely, this year will be better than last.

Gardens give me blank canvases that I can tweak every year, to design and create, with different colors and plant combinations. I find many small moments of joy there.

Garden soil connects me to mother earth; in return I try to pay homage to her by improving the soil, adding compost, horse and chicken manure, and not using synthetic fertilizers or pesticides.

Gardening has taught me that each year is different and helped me to accept change. One year the cucumbers thrive, the next they are decimated by cucumber beetles. Accept the rhythms, the ebb and flow.

Gardens offer surprise, giving me plant combinations I don't ask for, this year: hollyhock, nepeta, and comfrey.

To listen more carefully—the great horned owls calling to each other, the wind rustling in the trees, deer snorting in the woods. And to see where the moon rises, the brilliant green of new growth on the trees, frost on cabbage leaves.

Gardens encourage experimentation. One year I tried and failed to grow globe artichokes. This year I am trying fava beans. It is how I learn.

To respect the elders. We have a straggly native dogwood next to the house, which I was tempted to remove and replace with something young and healthy. "Let it live out its life," said my husband.

Praise to the raccoon who half a dozen times tripped and escaped from two sizes of have-a-heart traps—and took the container of dog food with him.

What Things Left Behind Say About a Home's Past, and the Times We Live In

We live in an old log house with big square beams, twisted staircases, and a double stone fireplace. The floor boards creak, dust falls through the ceilings, and the house is drafty, despite having been built at the bottom of three hills out of the wind. It sits on a county road, now abandoned, and since 1942 has been occupied by only two families.

It is a type of house few live in anymore, built by hardworking women and men who came to this western Pennsylvania outpost in much harder times, many years before we arrived here in 1988. I am grateful they did.

But who built this house, and when? We've assumed it's from roughly 1860. But we've never been sure, and finding out has not been easy. Our county recorder of deeds got me as far back as 1913. A 1964 tax assessment read, "old, remodeled house." I've spoken to a log house expert, a local historian, and dated our apple trees to the mid-nineteenth century, but still I've come up short.

Then I found my answer by means I didn't expect.

I invited two archaeologists, Tom and Pat Baker, a husband-and-wife team, to the barn one night to help me identify the random objects I've found scattered across the fields and forests over thirty-seven years: pottery shards, bits of glass, iron tools, farm equipment, shotgun shells, oyster shells, animal bones—and, of course, plastic.

I gathered up these artifacts to clean up the land, but also to give me clues about those who came before us: how they lived and farmed, what they ate and drank, the utensils they used, the area's industrial past. Mine is a commonplace collection; despite living in a town on the Pennsylvania frontier where the French and Indian War was fought, I've never found a musket ball or an arrowhead. And while I may use a fancy word and call these items artifacts, the truth is, much of what I have found was probably trash.

Settlers in rural America had no garbage collection, so they threw rubbish into pits outside summer kitchens. Or into privies or bottle dumps. They burned trash or tossed it into a pigsty. "People put waste products into a manure spreader and spread it over the fields," Tom said.

Out in the field, I've picked up a ceramic smoking pipe, likely from 1895, the mangled wood and metal heel of a shoe, and, turning the compost pile, I found a white, opaque piece of milk glass. "I rarely see that," Pat said. It turned out that a couple of towns over, a manufacturer of milk glass, the Westmoreland Glass Company, was founded in 1889.

Last year on a hike, I found a pitted, brown rock in the middle of a path. I thought it might be a meteorite. It turned out to be a piece of slag.

Had an iron furnace been on the property, Tom asked? Iron furnaces are abundant in this valley, but not here, at least to my knowledge. I know from an 1876 map that a tannery and a blacksmith shop were close by, but the slag, according to Pat, wouldn't have originated in either of those places. "That piece of slag is indicative of iron smelting and would have come from nearby coke ovens or an iron furnace," she said.

Nondescript pieces of glass suddenly come alive when archaeologists look at them. A clear shard with raised numbers and letters turned out to be a bottle embossed with a drugstore's name and address. A seam running along the neck of a pale blue bottle indicated it was handblown into a mold in the mid-to-late 1800s. A piece of brown glass was from an old Clorox bottle from the 1930s. Brown glass, I learned, kept light from altering the chemicals and indicated that the contents were poisonous.

I found an abundance of redware and stoneware, the everyday pottery used in this old house. Most of the stoneware was glazed brown and white, but one piece had a blue sponge pattern, probably from the early 1900s. A fragment of flow-blue refined earthenware, from about 1840 to 1900, had split into three from being burned. Pat put the plate back together like a puzzle.

And then came the revelation: Pat was able to date this property according to the pottery we didn't have. "Your collection is completely missing delftware, creamware, and pearlware," she said, listing pottery types that were common in North America from colonial times until the middle of the 1800s. "This tells me that your property was not occupied until the mid-1850s." I still don't know who built the house, but that is the closest I've come to accurately dating the place.

Wire nails backed up her assertion. I've found a lot of metal: half a set of tongs for grabbing hay bales or ice, a double bit ax, what might be an ox shoe, a vise and assorted hooks, screws, nuts, bolts, and wire nails. Wire nails were not manufactured until 1857, so that also suggested the house had not been lived in until then.

Not all the items I collected were trash, however. Some were lost, misplaced, or dropped. "They didn't see it fall off a saddle if they were on horseback," Tom said.

We, too, are guilty of inadvertently leaving items out in the environment. I've dropped plant tags, terra-cotta shards, and rubber bands. Tools fall off our ATV or out of our pockets. Machinery breaks in the field. I've come home from hikes with electric fence insulators, lawn mower wheels, chain from a manure spreader, and bungee cords. Sometimes, I get lucky and it's exactly the piece we were looking for and machinery can be fixed or a horseshoe put back on.

But we don't purposely toss trash into the woods. "Today, people find a ravine and dump it," Tom said, which is exactly what someone is doing at a deserted corner of the farm. They're throwing garbage from their car over a guardrail into a ravine. Not only common household trash, but hundreds of beer cans stuffed into red, plastic bags. One now hangs from a maple sapling like a giant red Christmas ornament.

Our county has no plastic bag ban and convenience stores, gas stations, and grocery stores hand them out for free.

I seldom drive that road but noticed the garbage when biking there, seven miles up steep hills with hairpin turns in the Allegheny Mountains, then down onto the flat by fields of cut hay and a sheep farm, where I often see a leucistic hawk. My ride borders woods where I pick morels and black raspberries and an enormous snapping turtle suns itself by a pond.

One day, I collected about a hundred items of trash, including soda and water bottles, French fry boxes, supersize cups, lottery tickets, straws, plastic tubs, power drink cans, and two containers of hypodermic needles. I saw a diaper down a different ravine but couldn't reach it.

I try to be understanding because this small township still has no municipal trash collection. It costs money to collect garbage. But I feel less kindly toward the appearance of the synthetic innards of an entire couch, packaging from morning-after pills, and, halfway down the ravine, an air purifier.

All this, despite dumping being illegal, with hefty fines and possible community service. But why pay someone to haul it away? There are no consequences.

I shudder to think of black bears, opossums, raccoons, and coyotes drinking from a stream riddled with broken glass and walking steep hillsides covered in rusty, jagged metal. Of birds picking through fast food wrappers and chipmunks nibbling on plastic containers. How the trash contaminates the air, water, and soil and affects the growth of native plants. And all the plastic running downstream.

And I can't help but wonder: Is this the archaeology of the future, the things we are leaving the next generation to study?

What will those artifacts tell them about us? About us all?

The Springhouse

I LOVE OUTBUILDINGS: SPRINGHOUSES, WOODSHEDS, BARNS, COTTAGES, AND tractor sheds. I'd have more if I could—a tool shed, a sugar house, a summer kitchen, a cider house. We have a small wooden building we call a goat shed because once we housed goats there. When the children were young, I wanted to convert a corn crib into a playhouse. (Sadly, I never got around to it.) On a trip to Vermont, we saw an outbuilding filled with old maps. A map house! If my husband had his way, he'd have one of those and a stone folly at the top of the hill.

Most outbuildings were simple structures—form ever following function, to paraphrase architect Louis Sullivan—used for practical purposes: to make maple syrup, press apples, cook during the hot months, or split wood. In his book, *FARM: The Vernacular Tradition of Working Buildings,* David Larkin explained the origin of early American outbuildings. When Europeans first came to America, settlers had to learn new ways of farming far away from the communal villages to which they'd become accustomed. Our landscape was vast and neighbors were distant so farmers had to be even more self-sufficient. "The farms they built reflect this," Larkin wrote. "In addition to a farmhouse and a barn, many outbuildings were built to accommodate the different activities of the isolated farmer."

One of the first tasks of early settlers was to find water—for themselves and their livestock. That usually meant a natural spring, hence the springhouse—a building so important that it was likely the first building constructed on a farm and indicated the location of the house and barn.

We have a springhouse on this farm, a simple cement building with clapboard at the gable, likely rebuilt since the mid-nineteenth century. It has a door and two windows and is nestled into the base of a hill, as many were. The building is painted white with green trim, matching the rest of the farmstead, and it is one story, but some had second stories to be used as living quarters or for other tasks, such as making butter. Ours is not beautiful, though many were, especially those made of stone or wood with cedar-shake roofs.

We have no moss on the roof, but according to Eric Sloane in *An Age of Barns*, "moss was encouraged because it helped to keep such buildings cool." Springhouses were also surrounded by trees, often willows which offered protection from the sun. We had a spectacular maple next to the springhouse, likely standing when the springhouse was built, which we just lost. Now, there's an oak—stately, but younger—that shades the structure. I've also found glass and pottery shards around the springhouse, so it might have been a spot where settlers threw their garbage.

Springhouses were built directly on top of a spring or next to it. Ours is next to the spring, which is tucked inside a moss-covered stone enclosure. A wooden door with old iron hinges keeps the animals and debris out. Once we had a ladle there to sip the spring's pure, cool water—a gourd hanging near the spring was customary for dipping—but that has disappeared. I will fix that.

Our drinking water comes from the farm's springs—the best water I've ever tasted. When we bought this farm thirty-eight years ago, we found, tacked to a basement wall, a handwritten note from the previous owner explaining the two ways that the water entered the house—one from the springhouse and the other from a spring located underneath the dining room. It's all rather mysterious, a convoluted scheme I barely understand and one of the difficulties of living in an old log house. Still, the springs have never let us down, but I do worry about them running dry as summer droughts occur more frequently.

Springhouses were nature's way to keep food cool, a forerunner to the icebox and the refrigerator. Water was piped from the spring into a trough inside the springhouse where earthenware crocks of milk, cheese, butter, cider and other foodstuffs were placed directly into the water. There may also have been shelves and hooks to hang other food items that needed cooling.

Spring water never freezes. That's because the water is deep, the flow constant, and it is warmed by the heat of the earth, rocks, and minerals. "Spring water maintains a temperature of around 53 degrees," said Theresa Gay Rohall, executive director of the Ligonier Valley Historical Society and the Compass Inn Museum. On December 15th of last year, I tested her theory. The outside temperature was 7 degrees with a below zero wind chill. I opened the springhouse door and saw a leaf or two and some spider webs, but otherwise clear, clean water. I dipped a thermometer into the spring: 50 degrees.

In *Foxfire 4*, the series of books that began in 1966 about Appalachian life, is a section about springhouses. Harry Brown in Georgia said he preferred a springhouse because it didn't take on the smell of fish as a refrigerator might. But Aunt Arie Carpenter in North Carolina said going to the springhouse required too many unnecessary steps to fetch her milk and butter, and it forced her outside in the rain. "I wouldn't trade one Frigidaire for a thousand springhouses," she said.

Myths and superstitions surround springhouses. Amos Long, Jr. wrote in *The Pennsylvania German Family Farm* that:

> *"To have healthy feet, one must bathe them in the water from a spring every evening."*
>
> *"Dip the hands and feet of the newborn infant into spring water and it will never suffer frost hands or feet."*
>
> *"When an infant is born, the first thing it is fed should be water fetched from the spring in a thimble. Then it will not be constipated."*
>
> *"If there is no bullfrog in the springhouse, the water isn't good."* (I have seen no bullfrog in the springhouse…)

Long has chapters on every type of outbuilding common to Pennsylvania Germans, including the icehouse, the pigpen, the carriage house, the smokehouse, the privy and some I'd never heard of: the malthouse, the sheepfold, the limekiln and the dryhouse.

Such buildings may be simple and functional, but to me they are more than that; they are aesthetically pleasing, an improvement to any rural landscape. But as we've grown accustomed to life's modern conveniences—not walking outside in the rain to fetch our milk, for instance—springhouses have lost their usefulness. They are falling into disrepair and disappearing from our environment—a way of life not coming back.

Still, I'll look for springhouses on my travels and take pleasure in their beauty. In doing so, I will remember a way of life more difficult, perhaps, but one more tied to the earth.

A malthouse, maybe?

Digging Basil's Grave

We buried Basil with his head facing east so that every day he could watch the sun rise.

The night our fifteen-year-old goldendoodle died, I lay on the floor next to him, flanked by our other two dogs. I stroked his hair and talked to him as he breathed his last breath. Our vet said it was the kind of death all pet owners want but few get. I know how fortunate I was to have been with him, at home, when he died. I covered him with a white sheet.

The next day my husband asked me to pick a spot on the farm to bury Basil. I looked downhill from our front porch and chose a place on the edge of the woods so that we could see him every day. My husband got the tools from the barn. The day was cold, thirty-one degrees with snow showers. Occasionally the sun poked out. But previous days had been warm so we were up to our ankles in mud, which made digging and back-filling slow and backbreaking. Each shovelful was heavy. My husband is strong, but still, I don't know how he did what he did. I looked over at him frequently—sopping wet and filthy and freezing. I marveled at his determination. I'm not sure I'd have continued without his resolve. I tried to spell him often, but I wasn't much help. I could barely lift the digging bar.

I longed for a backhoe. We could have hired someone with machinery, I thought. We could have called for help. Where were our children—our tall, strong children? Another reason I wished they didn't live so far away.

I opted for easier tasks that day, like cutting back sprigs of just-emerging poison ivy, multiflora rose, and stinging nettle—silly really, as they will probably come back stronger. But I told myself I wanted Basil to have a better view of the house. I weeded around the foxglove and Joe Pye weed so that later in the year he'd be surrounded by flowers. I hoisted rocks out of the muck and set them aside and saved shards of long-buried pottery and glass. Still, I dug enough that I could barely move the next day—no amount of modern-day exercise prepared my body for grave digging. It took over four and a half

nonstop hours to dig a hole four feet by four feet and three feet deep.

We buried him with his collar, which had his name and our phone number printed on it, and a tennis ball. My husband dug out of the ground a large, semicircular rock to use as a headstone. He rolled it into place. We said goodbye.

If we are lucky, we survive our pets, but losing them is brutal.

But when I look back on that day now, I think of it as beautiful. The intense physical activity was part of the healing process; it comforted me to have worked so hard to give Basil a nice transition to his next world. I was glad not to have used heavy machinery. I was glad not to have had help from strangers. My husband and I did it ourselves and we did it together. We'd kept Basil with us. I can walk out to his grave now, pat the dirt, and tell him I miss him.

The day after we buried Basil, I went out onto our front porch. I am a gardener and I might have known where the sun is at any time of day, but sun position had never occurred to me in the midst of burying him. It was 5 p.m. and the winter sun was fading. At the very moment I looked over at his grave, I saw, to my astonishment, a ray of light shining on Basil's headstone. Almost everything around it was dark.

The grave marker looked like a standing stone—sacred and ancient and aligned with the setting sun. It connected the earth to the sky and us to Basil, wherever he was. I knew then that his spirit would continue to bless this farm and those of us still here. And, like all the animals who've made our lives happier over many years, his sweet soul would remain part of this small patch of earth, always.

Bibliography

Browning, Frank. *Apples*. North Point Press, 1998.

Bunker, John. *Apples and the Art of Detection: Tracking Down, Identifying and Preserving Wild Apples*. 2019.

Burkett, Charles, Frank Stevens, and Daniel Hill. *Agriculture for Beginners*. Ginn and Company, 1903, 1904, 1914.

Carroll, David M. *The Year of the Turtle: A Natural History*. St. Martin's Griffin, 1991.

Carson, Rachel. *Silent Spring and Other Writings on the Environment*. Library of America, 2018.

Doyle, Arthur Conan. "The Adventure of the Blanched Soldier." A short story published in *Liberty Magazine*, 1926.

Larkin, David. *FARM: The Vernacular Tradition of Working Buildings*. The Monacelli Press, 1995.

Long, Jr., Amos. *The Pennsylvania German Family Farm*. The Pennsylvania German Society, 1972.

Lopez, Barry, and Gwartney, Debra, editors. *Home Ground: A Guide to the American Landscape*. Trinity University Press, 2006, 2013.

Magan, Manchan. *Thirty-Two Words for Field: Lost Words of the Irish Landscape*. Gill Books, 2020.

McDowell, Marta. *Emily Dickinson's Gardens: A Celebration of a Poet and Gardener*. McGraw-Hill, 2005.

Pope, Clifford. *Turtles of the United States and Canada*. Alfred A. Knopf, 1939.

Sheldrake, Merlin. *Entangled Life: How Fungi Make Our Worlds, Change Our Minds, and Shape Our Futures*. Random House, 2021.

Simard, Suzanne. *Finding the Mother Tree: Discovering the Wisdom of the Forest*. Vintage Books, 2021.

Sloane, Eric. *An Age of Barns*. Ballantine Books, 1967.

Stuart-Smith, Sue. *The Well-Gardened Mind: The Restorative Power of Nature*. Scribner, 2020.

Thoreau, Henry David. *Walden*. Yale University Press, 2004.

Thoreau, Henry David. *Wild Apples*. Applewood Books, 2015.

White, Gilbert. *The Natural History of Selborne*. Oxford University Press, 2013.

Wigginton, Eliot (Ed.). *Foxfire 4: Fiddle Making, Spring Houses, Horse Trading, Sassafras Tea, Berry Buckets, Gardening*. Anchor Books, 1977.

Wohlleben, Peter. *The Hidden Life of Trees: What They Feel, How They Communicate—Discoveries from a Secret World*. Greystone Books, 2016.

About the Author

Daryln Brewer Hoffstot is a freelance writer whose work has appeared in *The New York Times*, *The Boston Globe*, *The Philadelphia Inquirer*, and *Pittsburgh Quarterly*, among other publications. Her essay in *The New York Times*, "On a Pennsylvania Farm, Nature Is Not Just Carrying On," won a Notable Mention in *The Best American Science and Nature Writing 2021*. She won a 2024 Science/Environment award from the Western Press Club for her essay "What Would Rachel Carson Say?"

www.ingramcontent.com/pod-product-compliance
Ingram Content Group UK Ltd.
Pitfield, Milton Keynes, MK11 3LW, UK
UKHW041841010926
8329IPUK00002B/2

9 780811 778299